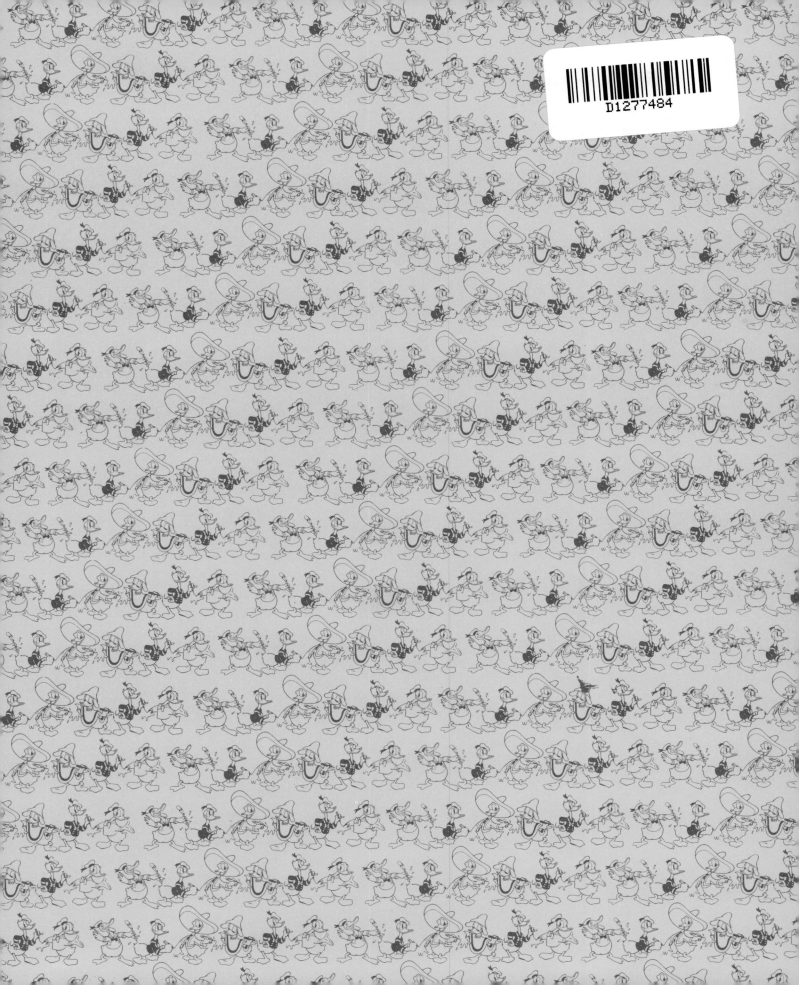

Walt Disney's DONALD DUCK

50 YEARS OF HAPPY FRUSTRATION

HPBooks®

First published in the United States
in 1984 by HPBooks®,
P.O. Box 5367, Tucson, AZ 85703. (602/888-2150)

ISBN: 0-89586-333-2
Library of Congress Catalog Card
Number: 84-80405

Created, designed and produced by
Three Duck Editions Limited,
P.O. Box 287, London N.1., England.

For Three Duck Editions:
Text: Flora O'Brien
Research: Justin Knowles and
Leslie Posner
Editor: Charlotte Parry-Crooke
Design: David Pearce
Production: Nick Facer

For HPBooks®:
Publisher: Rick Bailey
Editorial Director: Randy Summerlin
Editor: Judith Schuler

Typeset by Accent Graphics, London
Printed and bound in Hong Kong
by Mandarin Offset

CONTENTS

PREFACE

As with the creation of Donald Duck, no single person is responsible for the preparation of this book. Keith Bales' concept for a book, developed by Charlotte Parry-Crooke, David Pearce and myself over several months, was accomplished through the efforts of an enthusiastic production team, ably supported by significant outside contributors.

This book would not have existed without the encouragement and commitment of executives from Walt Disney Productions, in particular Wendall Mohler, Wayne Morris, Don MacLaughlin and Bob Ogden of the USA, Armand Bigle of Paris and Keith Bales of London. As a small independent publisher, I am grateful both for their guidance and for their support of my publishing philosophy. During my visits to Burbank, Wayne Morris and the knowledgeable Director of Archives, David R. Smith, provided invaluable and continual assistance. Mary Holoboff, Pat Lawson, Rose Motzko, Paula Sigman, Jeanette Steiner and Carson Van Osten gave additional, and welcome, support.

Special interviews were generously given by Ward Kimball and Clarence "Ducky" Nash, whose "Duck Language" successfully tangled our tapes! Bernard C. Shine was a significant consultant on Donald merchandise. He allowed items from his fine collection to be photographed by Marvin Meister. Bruce Hamilton, of Another Rainbow Publishing, generously provided information and transparencies of "Barks art," including Barks' 50th birthday painting, "*A 1934 Belchfire Runabout!*"

Book production was undertaken on short notice. During production, the spirit of Donald created a special form of involvement, fun and much "happy frustration!" Among those who succumbed to Donald's unavoidable charisma, and whom I should like to thank for their contributions, are Flora O'Brien for her perceptive text, David Pearce for his vibrant graphic design, Leslie Posner for her efficient research and Charlotte Parry-Crooke for her committed editorial control. Other supporting members of the English "Duck Team" included Nick Facer, Cath Pettyfer, Liz James and Michelle Perry. I also want to thank HPBooks for its sustained co-publishing commitment, especially Paul Clauser for his project coordination.

This book is a tribute to Donald Duck and to those who participated in his evolution. Let us hope it will inspire those who will take his development yet further during the next 50 years to join this particular "Duck Team" in saying "Thank Goodness for Donald Duck!"

Justin Knowles
Three Duck Editions
London 1984

INTRODUCTION

Fifty years ago, the world's most famous duck made his film debut. On June 9, 1934, Donald Duck appeared in a Disney short called *The Wise Little Hen*, and since that historic occasion, he has not looked back. His rapid rise to fame, if not fortune, is unparalleled in the history of the cinema. He once declared his annual income as $2,501! Within a year of his classic performance in *The Band Concert* in 1935, he challenged the better-natured Mickey Mouse as Disney's top cartoon personality.

His influence has been global. He has starred in 128 Donald Duck cartoons and appeared in 42 other shorts and features. His movies have been shown in 76 countries, and television has provided an outlet for his temper in 29 countries. Donald Duck comic strips are published in over 100 newspapers outside the USA, and Donald Duck comic books are distributed in 47 countries. In 1960, Dell Comics estimated his circulation at 15 million while newspaper comic strips and Sunday color pages hit 28 million.

Donald's cartoons have won 25 film awards, including an Oscar in 1943 and 11 other Academy Award nominations. His fan mail remains prodigious. Not without reason have Tony Hiss and David McClelland called him "the most universally popular figment of the human imagination."

We have all been amused and fascinated by this web-footed wonder. Made up of numerous artistic components and cinematographic processes, he is one of animation's most successful illusions of life. But Donald transcends technicalities. He is visually exciting, with a vital, tangible body and a psyche that communicate strongly with adults as well as children. His zany personality makes an immediate impact, and it is certainly no exaggeration to say that Donald has a life of his own.

Early in his career, Donald forced himself upon the world, and he demanded, gained and retained everyone's attention. He seemed determined to make himself known — and heard. He was a "real person," escaping the discipline and control that the Disney Studio normally exercised over other characters. Said Robert D. Feild, "No one has yet succeeded in suppressing Donald; in fact the Studio has had to surrender to his foibles, lest he make an even greater nuisance of himself."

Donald is a duck/man with an all-too-human nature. It is this which accounts for his mass appeal. We can all identify with his misdirected will to be in control, as well as the humor and pathos of his frustrations.

So, Donald Duck, you are 50 and a phenomenon. It is time to reassess you. After watching your antics for so many years, we would like to find out what makes you tick. This book is a tribute to your life and work and to the art of your creators. It examines your role as entertainer, and it considers your place in our culture. (Culture — *you* know about that!) Don't worry, it won't hurt a bit. We're going to take a closer look at you — purely for the fun of it.

THE BIRTH OF A DUCK NAMED DONALD

DONALD'S CREATORS: DISNEY AND DUCKY

Any investigation into Donald Duck's origins must begin with Walt Disney, the pioneer of film animation. In the 1930s and 1940s Walt was building a working environment with just the right atmosphere for a character like Donald to emerge and flourish.

In the early days of the Hyperion Avenue studios, which opened in 1926, Walt, his brother Roy and a handful of others looked after almost every aspect of the production of his popular, but comparatively primitive, cartoons of animals, flowers and trees. Oswald the Rabbit was his earliest success. But Disney himself was not really an animator. He soon hired artists who were better draftsmen than he. His great achievement was to lay the foundations for future animation.

Walt functioned best as an "idea man," with an unerring instinct for entertaining situations and what Jack Hannah, a former Disney director, called "a very, very good story mind." Disney wanted a cartoon to be more than a string of gags. "You have to go beyond getting a laugh," he said. "You have to have pathos in the thing." He also knew what pleased audiences and believed in giving the public what it wanted, while simultaneously striving for the highest possible standards in his medium. Though as conscious of budget limitations as Roy, the administrator, he was a perfectionist willing to throw out expensive footage if it did not please him and reshoot at the last moment. Disney shorts frequently cost two or three times more to produce than their equivalents at other studios.

In addition to being the producer of the first fully synchronized sound cartoon, Walt developed techniques such as the story board (see page 50). Its use became common practice in animation

Walt Disney, pioneer of film animation, and Donald Duck, one of Disney's most famous cartoon characters, are shown here in a 1954 photograph. Disney recognized Donald's potential and encouraged the Duck teams to bring out Donald's best — and his worst.

and publishing. One of his obsessions was the multiplane camera, for which a special Academy Award was won — "I always wanted a good camera." The film medium was revolutionized by the Disney development of the Xerox process for transferring drawings to celluloid. The color range used by Disney artists was vast, breathtaking and always far ahead of its time. Walt was also the first major Hollywood producer to work in television, where Donald joined him in the famous Duck-on-the-desk episodes.

Disney's skill as coordinator enabled him to bring out the best in people, encouraging them to work to their fullest capacity. He was good at recognizing talent and gathered it around him, always sensing the right man for a job and finding those best able to build what he envisioned. His interest in the personality of his animal creations and his continual striving for realistic surface also forced him into the role of educator. "We cannot do the fantastic things based on the real," he said, "unless we first know the real."

Ultimately, Walt was the standard-setter — things were either "Disney" or "un-Disney."

Walt was the first cartoon producer to appreciate the special talents of individual artists, and he allowed them to concentrate on what they did best. Donald Duck grew out of, and lent himself to, this experimental method. Walt recognized Donald's potential after his 1934 debut in *The Wise Little Hen*. Walt's own striving for expressive personality plus adherence to reality in many ways paralleled the development of the Duck.

Not surprisingly, it was Disney who decided to co-star the fractious Duck bit-player in the next Mickey Mouse cartoon, *Orphan's Benefit* (1934). The rest is history. But it is clear that Walt had been looking for a foil for Mickey for some time, and he had also been playing with the idea of a talking duck. This is borne out by the account — of which there are several versions — of his first encounter with Clarence "Ducky" Nash, who has been the voice of Donald Duck for 50 years.

In 1933, Clarence Nash was a milk delivery man with a talent for animal voice mimicry. The Adohr Milk Company, for which he drove a miniature milk wagon pulled by miniature horses, billed him as "Whistling Clarence, the Adohr Bird Man." On an impulse, Nash auditioned for Disney, impersonating baby chickens, turkeys and crickets. His *tour de force*, however, was a recitation in a baby goat voice, on which he had been

Donald's relatives invade the Studio. Enter Ludwig von Drake, Donald's dotty professor uncle, who was developed for television in 1961. Far left and below: In these 1961 photographs, Ludwig disrupts life in Walt Disney's office.

Above: "The Duck on the Desk." Donald gets the attention of the boss in one of his many television appearances in *Walt Disney Presents*.

working for years, of *Mary Had a Little Lamb*. Everyone cheered so the story goes.

"Stop!" cried Disney. "That's our talking duck!"

"Our talking *duck*?" said Ducky. "*Our* talking duck?"

Another rendition of the story tells how Walt discovered Clarence on a local radio show and sought him out. Still another maintains Disney's initial reaction to the inimitable quacky voice was that if ever they needed a talking duck, Nash was the man for the job.

Whatever the details, Ducky signed a contract with Disney in December 1933 for a still-to-be-created character. In this respect Donald is unique. The initial drawings for his early films were developed from the voice of Clarence Nash. Disney encouraged Ducky to laugh or get angry in a duck voice, and Ducky practiced and perfected a range of emotions. In time, he also did the Nephews' voices and Daisy's — one octave higher. Ducky's versatility has progressed so far that he now dreams of one last film in which Donald will do nothing but sing grand opera!

The dynamite duo — Donald and Clarence "Ducky" Nash, photographed together in 1969. Ducky has been Donald's inimitable voice for 50 years.

Jack Hannah was originally a Donald story man. He later directed some of the best Donald Duck cartoons. Here, Hannah, Ducky and Donald inspect a sequence of preliminary cartoon sketches called a story board. See page 50.

Disney and Nash were not the only creators. Others share the responsibility and credit for developing the world's most cantankerous and entertaining Duck. Directors, animators, story men, comic book and comic strip artists and writers all played a part in Donald's evolution.

Dick Lundy was the animator of *Orphan's Benefit* (1934), in which Donald made his second, and decisive, appearance. Lundy confessed, "I listened to the dialogue track and decided that he was an ego-show-off. If anything crossed him, he got mad and blew his top." Though animators Art Babbitt and Dick Huemer first drew Donald, Lundy was largely responsible for the Duck's early screen personality.

Donald's development also owes much to the imaginations and inventive genius of Carl Barks and Jack Hannah, who worked together as story men on 27 cartoons during the classic era of Donald shorts. Most of these were directed between 1937 and 1947 by Jack King. Barks and Hannah helped concoct a series of bizarre, hilarious plots that gave unprecedented scope to Donald's penchant for pandemonium. With King directing, Barks and Hannah produced some of the best Donald shorts ever made. Hannah later became a director, first introducing the troublesome chipmunks, Chip and Dale, then an assortment of other nuisances to serve as antagonists to Donald. He was also instrumental in bringing Donald to television, allowing the public to enjoy several riotous Duck dramas.

Director Jack Kinney's broad, brisk approach to comedy was perfect for *Der Fuehrer's Face* (1943), the Academy Award-winning film that brought out Donald's true grit. In this film Donald was pitted against no less an adversary than Hitler's entire war machine. Story

Top left: A Duck team
at work. This 1937
photograph shows Carl
Barks — who later
became the great
comic book artist —
with other members of
the Disney Story
Department. As Barks
points to the relevant
frame on the story
board, Harry Reeves,
then the head of the
Story Department, acts
out different roles.
Good Scouts (1938) is
the Donald cartoon
under discussion.

Bottom left: Ducky
Nash and puppet
Donald inspect an
animation drawing of
Donald and one of the
infamous chipmunks
(see page 43). Certain
animators had a flair
for Donald and worked
exclusively on his
films. Bill Justice is
shown here at his
drawing board.

Ducky and Donald
continue a tour of the
Studio. Left: Here,
they take a closer look
at a "cel" of Donald
with Chip and Dale.
The cel is positioned
under the camera,
ready to be photo-
graphed onto film.
See page 55.

man Dick Kinney also worked with
Hannah, and this duo was famous for the
vigorous gags and the fast pacing of films
such as *No Sail* (1945) and *Frank Duck
Brings 'Em Back Alive* (1946).

On February 7, 1938, Donald starred
in his own strip on the pages of the daily
newspaper, drawn by Al Taliaferro and
scripted by Bob Karp. Taliaferro went on
to draw the Donald Duck daily comic
strip for over 30 years, and Karp scripted
it until 1974. These two men formed
another indomitable Duck team.

During World War II, Carl Barks left
the Disney Studio and worked solo on
Donald Duck comic books. Barks created
new and preposterous predicaments and
introduced a new family of ducks (see
page 35), all based on the original
Donald. Now retired, Barks has
immortalized his Duck creations with oil
on canvas and has produced hundreds of
highly sought-after Duck masterpieces.
Barks has been with Donald from almost
the beginning, having joined the Studio in
1935. He has become known as the
"Duck Master." His contribution to
Donald's evolution can be seen in his
vast, innovative output of work.

DONALD HIMSELF
DEVELOPING DONALD'S PHYSIQUE

Donald's dynamic expressiveness and physical versatility stunned the audiences of the early shorts. Below left: In *Mickey's Circus* (1936), Donald exhibits his growing penchant for pandemonium.

Below right: Donald as he first appeared in *The Wise Little Hen* (1934). With long bill and knobby knees, Donald's form was primitive and static by comparison to his flexible physique of later years.

Donald is so amusing, and his transitions of feeling and movement so rapid, his audience is seldom aware what makes his antics so engaging. Like all great entertainers, Donald relieves us of thought by substituting recognition, surprise or emotion. But an examination of his physical form, his personality and his character (see page 20) reveals the secrets behind the dazzling effect Donald produces.

With a combination of cuddliness and feistiness, ducks are inherently funny, and Donald is physically true to his species. He has the duck's distinctive shape, quack and waddle. With the exception of his hands, he is more like a duck, in body and behavior, than Mickey a mouse or Goofy a dog. He also has the visually satisfying pear shape of his kind and is always drawn as one piece rather than two parts. Animation tricks, such as keeping the leg well up into the body and showing the sag beneath, emphasize the sense of his weight. He is short and squatty, yet highly flexible, as though made of some rubbery material. And he has tangibility — he is a touchable duck — plus a resilience that allows him to be stretched, squeezed and twisted into truly fantastic postures.

Said Jack Hannah, "You could rough him up and the next minute he was happy as the devil. He changed *that* fast." This capacity for exaggeration makes him the most active and versatile of all the Disney characters. His fast and furious physical changes are an expression of his excitable nature. His dynamism and invigorating qualities are transferred to the audience. This combination of substance and mobility is gratifying to watch. Donald is sensual but not sexual.

Disney himself summed it up. "Donald's got a big mouth, big belligerent eyes, a twistable neck and a substantial backside that's highly flexible. The Duck comes near being the animator's ideal subject. He's got plasticity plus!"

In his first film appearance in *The Wise Little Hen* in 1934, Donald was an angular, domestic duck. He had an orange bill and feet, white feathers and a blue sailor suit and hat. His bill was longer and his body plumper than in later years, and he had feathery fingers rather than hands. The classic Donald was not perfected until

the late 1930s. The critical year for Donald's physique was 1936, for it was then, between *Mickey's Grand Opera* and *Moving Day*, that Donald acquired his new shorter bill and more human, if improbable, hands.

Characteristic gestures made audiences anticipate outbursts of Donald's titanic temper — the narrowing of his eyes or the notorious "fighting pose," invented by Dick Lundy for *Orphan's Benefit* (1934). The "fighting pose" was subsequently used whenever Donald reached the extremity of frustration. "For this I had him lean forward, chin out, arm straight out and fisted, the other arm, with fist, was swaying back and forth," said Lundy. "His one foot was out straight, heel on floor, the other foot under him as he hopped up and down, quacking. The action was fairly violent for the time."

"Plasticity plus." The twistable, bendable, stretchable, shakable, but 100 per cent unbreakable Donald Duck! Left: Donald performs in a tennis tournament in *Walt Disney's Donald Duck*, published around 1938 by the English firm, Birn Brothers. Below: Donald executes some very fancy footwork in *Hockey Champ* (1939).

Every part of Donald, even his clothes, has always been exploited by animators to convey the intensity of his reactions. His eyes are kept to the side of his head so that more black can be used for expression. His bill curves into his circular head when he smiles or protrudes on the outside when he frowns or gets mad. His head is usually kept smooth, but when his dander is up, so are his top feathers. When he is pleased, his wagging tail shows his character, but the tail does not wiggle when he is angry. Donald's jacket is kept loose to help the flow of animation, but it is his hat that is particularly effective. During his rare moments of composure, it sits straight on his head with the ribbon at the back. When he is angry, it drops down over his eyes and the ribbon flaps in front. When he is surprised or frightened, it flies right off his head.

These physical contrivances, and many others, express the personality of the indomitable Duck, for Donald is a fully integrated creature whose body and soul are one.

Some of Donald's physical intricacies and a rich variety of Duck expressions. Animators and comic book artists referred to both physical and psychological model sheets and style sheets, like those shown here, once Donald had developed his full form and character.

FEAR

WORRY

SHOUTING

JOY

GREED

FRUSTRATION

SLEEPINESS

WONDER

ACCUSATION

COMMAND

REBELLION

Early in Donald's career, the Disney Story Department found the Duck was good "provided he played true to character," but that he could not be funny if a situation did not fit his idiosyncrasies. Consequently, gags were always a natural outgrowth of his personality. The inevitability of every catastrophic episode in a Donald Duck cartoon is rooted in his fractious nature. Audiences can be secure in anticipating the worst, because Donald is Donald whether he plays a mechanic, a suitor or a truant officer.

From the feckless fellow of *The Wise Little Hen* (1934), Donald's character broadened and deepened to become as complex as any human's. "The Duck was very versatile to work with. Donald could be anything. He had every emotion a human being had. He could be cute, mischievous, go warm or cool at any moment," said Jack Hannah.

Epithets of both critics and audience reflect the rich tapestry of Duck psychology: cocky, reckless, perverse, gullible, awkward, strident, boastful, disreputable, jaunty, gallant, grumbling, flexible, obstinate, cowardly, heroic. In addition, he has been labeled upstart, exhibitionist, egomaniac, credulous blunderer, spokesman for the weak and oppressed and symbol of capitalist imperialism — such is his multi-dimensional persona. And he is certainly not inhibited. He articulates anger, despair, bitterness, hope, pleasure and dreams, forever exposing himself, forever giving himself away. Donald may be a *bona fide* hysteric, but he is a liberated hysteric, completely unrepentant in his mania.

Donald's most-notorious trait is his temper. A creature of strong desires, he knows what he wants and is determined to get it. When

thwarted, he blows his stack. That is why he is always given a problem to solve or a goal to fight for. The obstacle to his gratification may be animate or inanimate — both have proved equally successful in rousing his fury.

Nothing brings out the best or worst in Donald like an insurmountable challenge. Either he loses his temper or counters with a vigor and tenacity that brook no interference. This was how the Disney Story Department described him in 1939. "The Duck never compromises. Regardless of the odds against him, he comes back again and again to the fray, each time more determined than before, and rants and kicks and punches and yanks until either he or the opposition is in ruins." Beneath this obstinate disregard for consequences lie a valor that demands respect and a boldness we are forced to admire. The Duck has pluck.

"Part of Donald's tragedy is that he engineers his own destruction through a compulsive need to prove himself," explained Carl Barks. Above: Donald is seen in a still from *Chips Ahoy* (1956). In this short, the Duck does battle with the mischievous chipmunks, Chip and Dale.

"Donald was always better *as* a problem that *at* one," said Marcia Blitz. Her point is illustrated by Donald's tussle with a broken xylophone (top right) in *Symphony Hour* (1942) and his unintentional arrival in a pelican's beak (right) in *Lighthouse Keeping* (1946).

Donald's alternative approach to problem-solving is an attempt to be sly or clever. "This requires strategy" is a typical remark. But he is no Machiavellian. He does not possess the intelligence or the malice required. He is essentially gullible, and his cunning invariably backfires.

A born actor, Donald has a strong ego and longs to be the center of attention. In his second two films, *Orphan's Benefit* (1934) and *The Band Concert* (1935), he was cast as the upstager, battling for the spotlight, playing the piccolo, singing, reciting poetry. "Nothing is more odious to Donald than to live in obscurity. Never will he accept a secondary role in life. But the poor fellow has no talent for success except in the realm of the ridiculous," said Vivian Moog in *Symbols of Our Times*.

Like all egocentrics, Donald continually sets himself up in situations that are bound to offend him. He is incredibly touchy and sensitive about himself. Ridicule is intolerable, his pride is easily injured and he can't take a joke. His sense of humor is not highly developed, though he is easily amused and enjoys a laugh at others' expense. But he is never vicious. There is a carefree element in his nature which always turns up fresh and ready for a fight or frolic. His lapses of temper are brief. Even his blackest moods find him ready to forgive, and he is easily mollified by a little gratification.

Donald "challenges the utmost bastions of reality," said Carl Barks. Right: As Donald's plane emerges from a cloud in *Flying Jalopy* (1943), he finds himself flying Ben Buzzard, another of his devious antagonists.

He is no hypocrite, just an honest straight forward nuisance. And he has, too, his tender moments.

Because there were so many facets to Donald's personality, he lent himself more to development than other cartoon characters and was saved from being type-cast as "Pest Personified."

Donald evolved. He threw fewer tantrums and smiled more often. He was made more engaging and even acquired some charm. By 1937, the process of humanization had begun. He became more sympathetic, trying to be good, despite his mischievous inclinations and volatile temper. Donald was never transformed into an altruist, but he always did his best to help friends in a fix, however ineptly.

"He has the greatest of all virtues: courage in the face of adversity," wrote Helen G. Thompson. Left: Donald shows his courage and fights for survival in an argument with a bee at the top of a city skyscraper in *Window Cleaners* (1940).

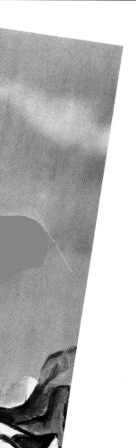

The Duck was a product of his era, and his character development parallels the sociological changes in America during the 1930s. Donald reflects the shift in population and values from rural to urban, leaving the barnyard to become a city dweller with a variety of jobs. In this respect, he had mass appeal as a struggling worker. He was a Depression Duck, hence some of his anger and resentment. He possessed a fighting spirit that ensures survival in difficult times, and this accounts for much of his early popularity.

Beginning life on a dilapidated houseboat where he lived ingloriously, a no-good hippy duck, his aquatic origins were inauspicious. But his fame and personality required a broader spectrum. "So Donald was given a house with its array of cantankerous gadgets...a lawn bedeviled with weeds and gophers, a car, a girlfriend," wrote Carl Barks. "He had become a duck-of-the-world and let the world know that he thought himself abused." Donald became more human, with human problems. He was working-man, taxpayer, even surrogate parent. A whole new spectrum of annoyances appeared before him. The Duck had moved to the Middle Class.

It was as Barks' comic book protagonist, however, that Donald underwent his ultimate humanization. More than anyone before him, Barks blurred the boundaries between duck and man. Moreover, he made Donald a hero, transporting him, along with his burgeoning family, into a realm of fantastic adventure. He has gone from Duckburg to the outer reaches of the galaxy. Where will it end? Perhaps, in another 50 years, we'll know.

The appeal of this "paraducksical" paragon has now been a subject of speculation for half a century. We know that tension is relieved through laughter, but Donald's brand of comedy seems to have a particularly therapeutic effect on audiences. He screams, squawks and jumps, and the audience experiences a physical and moral catharsis.

Above all, Donald is vital. He has enormous energy and fierce desires. Desire equals life, and energy equals life, but the animal and child that live in the man have been suppressed by social indoctrination. Donald's rages, in particular, are a manifestation of this vitality, and vitality exerts a strong attraction.

Both children and adults like excitement, and with Donald things happen at breakneck speed. Gag is heaped upon gag. Donald becomes a whirling ball of feathered fury. His adrenaline is transferred to the audience, who imbibes it, so to speak, by osmosis. He is particularly adored by children, to whom excitement is crucial. According to one survey by a child psychologist, children also love Donald because his character is constant. This offers psychological comfort because he can be

relied upon to act in a certain way, and he is seen by them as a totally reliable comrade in adventure.

Donald's appeal to adults is more complex. It is a tradition as old as Aesop and the totem that animal heroes can be used to make light of human foibles. Says teacher Katherine P. Hutchinson, "When we see our whims and petty vices in animal form, as in Donald Duck, they are funny, and, once recognized, we have already taken the first steps toward their correction." Obviously, Donald was never meant to serve as an example of moral rectitude, but the point is well understood.

In Donald we recognize our own perverseness. Because he's funny, we laugh at him and therefore at ourselves. Because we like him so much, we forgive him his faults. Simultaneously, we forgive ourselves and are purged of guilt. He reminds us that human beings are naughty by nature. Donald waddles along the razor-edged path of permissible

naughtiness. Ever the anarchist, he exemplifies the bad behavior in which we would all like to indulge if we could, but which society rarely permits. Donald is the ungovernable child, the mess-maker imprisoned in us all, and so we applaud loudly when the monster is allowed to rave with impunity.

Donald was by far the most aggressive star of the Disney pantheon, and he came as a surprise to contemporary audiences. But when Donald quacks "Wanna fight?" he is more frustrated than violent, and his rages seldom harm anyone. The outbursts are brief and usually directed against petty injustices or annoyance. When he does indulge in fisticuffs, it is as "Little Man" against "Big Menace," and his adversaries are always larger than himself. "The laughter Donald creates is not an incitement to violence, but rather an emotional sedative," said a 1952 Disney press release. His mistakes are blunders, not malicious, and we forgive

Helen G. Thompson described Donald as "an iconoclastic little fellow, bearing life's burdens and being one." Not surprisingly, Donald ends up causing a riot in *Magician Mickey* (1937), from which a scene is shown above.

him his faults because of his greater courage and gallantry.

For Donald is, in his wacky way, heroic. He is "a champion who will stand up and yell defiance and abuse at injustice and nagging provocations as they come to the common lot," the 1952 press release continued. In other words, Donald squawks for us all. In his impotent rage he is supremely vocal and is loved and approved *because* he squawks. It is the American way. Perhaps it is this outspoken bravery that, more than anything, endears him to us. As Robert D. Feild wrote in *The Art of Walt Disney*, "We have been obliged to overlook his precocity and to accept him as one of us because we recognize, particularly in his moments of despair, a gentle heroism that we would wish to emulate." He tries. Gosh, how he tries!

Donald speaks for the little man who can never get the better of a situation, and for the impotent and the frustrated. He voices his complaints and cries out against the bitterness of life with a courage they lack. He also speaks for every egomaniac bearing the burden of a secret greatness that has passed unnoticed. If he's frustrated, it's because life is frustrating. If he's exasperating, it's because he, too, is exasperated.

"Our true personalities are best revealed by reactions to a change we did not expect," said Frank Thomas and Ollie Johnston. Despite his good intentions (see pages 21 and 23), Donald is caught off guard and loses his cool in *Self Control* (1938).

Donald could not have been Donald without his unique voice. Clarence "Ducky" Nash, inventor and perfector of what has been called the most garrulous incoherence of all time, provided Disney with the soul of a character for which Disney, in turn, created a form.

Ironically, "Duck Talk," so distinctive in quality and so potent in effect, is 50 per cent unintelligible, which is why it is used sparingly in dialogue. It teases the listener, allowing him to understand just enough, and often skirting the strictures of early film censorship. Duck Talk has been compared to the "brekekkekex, co-ax, co-ax" of Aristophanes' *The Frogs*. Its rhythmic quality has been compared to the musical cry of a bird and described, by Robert D. Feild, as possessing "an inarticulate wisdom transcending the commonplace of language." This is interesting, because Ducky Nash claims vocal chords are not used in Duck Talk.

In spite of, or because of, these primal associations, Duck Talk is a highly successful mode of communication. However, it does present certain technical difficulties. Donald's voice is always recorded first, and his words and dialogue are carefully synchronized with his actions. The voice makes the character and often determines action, pose and gestures. Whenever possible, Donald pantomimes the dialogue, and special recording techniques are used for the different types of Duck dialogue, such as offstage, from a distance or confidential asides.

Certain sounds are problematic. For example, *s*, particularly a double *s*, produces too much sibilance. A *t* at the start of a word is lost or sounds as a *d*. To make the *o*, *u*, *y* and *w* sounds, animators have to distort the bill for a few frames.

Though Duck dialogue is most successful when sentences are kept short, the interjection of some large words, such as magnificent, relaxation, stupendous or predicament invariably provokes a laugh.

By 1939, Clarence Nash and the Disney Studio had raised Duck Talk to a fine art. Certain expressions and sentences were found to work particularly well, both in sound engineering and in conveying the Duck's personality, and they were catalogued in a studio memo. Here is a random sampling from *Practical Duck Expressions*. This is listed in full on page 96.

"Hey, what's the big idea?...I'll fix him!...Such ignorance!...Well, I'll be...Directions — phooey!...So, you're going to be obstinate, uh?...This is a fine predicament...Making a sap out of me...Absolutely exasperating!...Positively disgusting!...Bu...bu...(scared)...For me?...This is a fine situation...Hi, toots!...You big palooka!...See? Nothing to it!"

Donald always presented special technical problems. Recording his voice and dialogue was no exception. Left: Donald quacks in an illustration from *Walt Disney's Donald Duck — Express to Funland*, published in 1937 in England by Birn Brothers. Far left: Donald lets out a characteristic "Yeow!" in one of *Walt Disney's Comics and Stories*.

World War II thrust Donald into a new symbolic role. His anger, desperation and aggression more closely reflected the spirit of the times than those of any other Disney character. His spirit was the perfect representation of America's determination in the war effort. At last his belligerent nature had found an outlet that was not only acceptable but also honorable. Donald became patriotic citizen, soldier and even diplomat.

It all began with the shock of Pearl Harbor. On December 8, 1941, Disney was offered a government contract to produce 20 animated training films for the military. These were to deal with such topics as precision bombing and torpedo assembly, and they were all top secret.

By the summer of 1942, the Studio had more government commissions than it could cope with. By 1943, 94 per cent of its output was under government contract. 1943 saw the release of *Victory Through Air Power*, a theatrical feature that was eventually screened for Churchill, Roosevelt and the Joint Chiefs of Staff.

The Disney commitment to the Allied cause also resulted in a group of so-called

Right and below: Prepared! Along with other Hollywood stars, Donald heeded the call to arms and did his duty for his country. *The New Spirit* (1942) was a highly effective piece of propaganda. It persuaded millions of Americans to part with their tax dollars in support of the Allied cause.

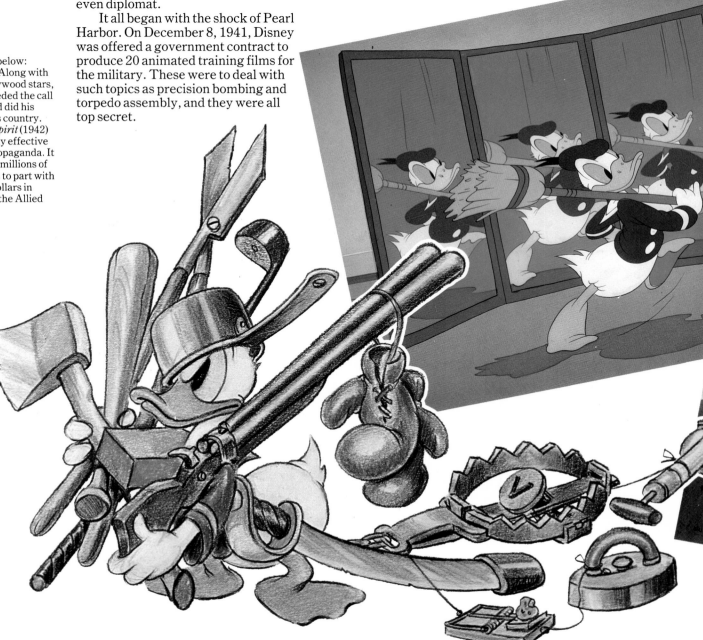

Left: Never had Donald's belligerence found a more legitimate outlet. His performance in the anti-Nazi short, *Der Fuehrer's Face* (1943), won the film an Academy Award. In this scene, Donald is put to work on a munitions assembly line.

"incentive" films. The third was made for the National Film Board of Canada in 1942 and marked Donald's debut as a solid citizen, exhorting audiences to buy war bonds. The Duck's good and bad selves do battle for his money, and Donald's higher nature triumphs.

Also in 1942, Donald starred in *The New Spirit*. The repercussions of this film were enormous and surprising. Recent legislation had created 7 million new American taxpayers who had never filed a tax return. The US Treasury Department was anxious to persuade all Americans that it was patriotic to pay taxes and to pay them quickly. Secretary of the Treasury Henry Morgenthau approached Disney early in 1942 with the idea of making a cartoon on this subject, utilizing a character who would portray "Mr Average Taxpayer." Morgenthau expressed surprise when Disney proposed Donald as the Duck for the job. Disney's response was that donating Donald to the Treasury was equivalent to MGM donating Clark Gable.

The complete Disney pantheon of stars made up a formidable "platoon" of patriots during the war. Left: Donald takes command of the infantry, while Mickey leads the regiment of tanks appearing over the horizon.

Tax returns were due on March 15, 1942. Despite the very difficult film deadline, *The New Spirit* was completed in less than a month and rushed to thousands of theaters across the country. In it Donald is cajoled and instructed by a talking radio that urges him to file his return immediately and tells him just how to do it. "Taxes to Beat the Axis" was the cartoon's slogan, and it proved a highly effective piece of propaganda. Over 32 million people saw the film, and a Gallup Poll reported than an amazing 37 per cent said that it had directly affected their willingness to pay their taxes. Critic Bosley Crowther of the *New York Times* called it "the most effective of the morale films yet released by the government."

Ironically, Disney was almost not paid the $80,000 owed for production costs. The House of Representatives vetoed his appropriation, regarding the film purely as entertainment and therefore of secondary financial importance to bombs. "Not a Dime for Disney" became a catch-phrase for the ensuing scandal in which Disney and Donald were unjustly accused of making money from the war. In fact, Walt had agreed at the start to do all his government films on a non-profit basis. The gesture was both patriotic and practical because it kept the Studio open during what would otherwise have been a fallow period.

In 1943, Morgenthau gave Disney $20,000 to rework *The New Spirit*. The result was a fresh cartoon segment spliced onto the latter half of the earlier film. In *The Spirit of '43*, Donald is torn between a zoot-suited spendthrift and a canny Scotsman, who bears an uncanny resemblance to Uncle Scrooge Mc Duck. Both try to get his money, which he ultimately surrenders to the Internal Revenue Service.

In *Donald Gets Drafted* (1942) the inevitable happens. Donald Fauntleroy Duck receives a greeting (number 13) from Uncle Sam on April 1, 1942. The story pits him against arch-fiend Peg Leg Pete, who turns up as Donald's top sergeant — with two good legs to boot. But unlike Daffy Duck in *Draftee Daffy* (1943), Donald is a willing inductee. As in *The Vanishing Private* and *Sky Trooper*, both made in 1942, Donald is the little man lost in the bewildering System, which does not, however, prevent him from asserting his individuality.

The year 1943 was a critical time for affairs on the European Front, and most of the 13 shorts released by Disney in that year referred directly to the war. Among them were the four anti-Nazi films which the Publicity Department called "Psychological Productions." *Education for Death*, *Reason and Emotion*, *Chicken Little* and *Der Fuehrer's Face* were all pointed attacks at the Third Reich. The last is a bitter satire on life in Hitler's Germany. Donald is a starved, oppressed worker on a munitions assembly line. He is again cast as the little man, but this time he is crushed and

Weighted-down by innumerable reference books and entwined in ticker tape, Donald thinks he will need all these items to fill out his tax form in *The New Spirit* (1942).

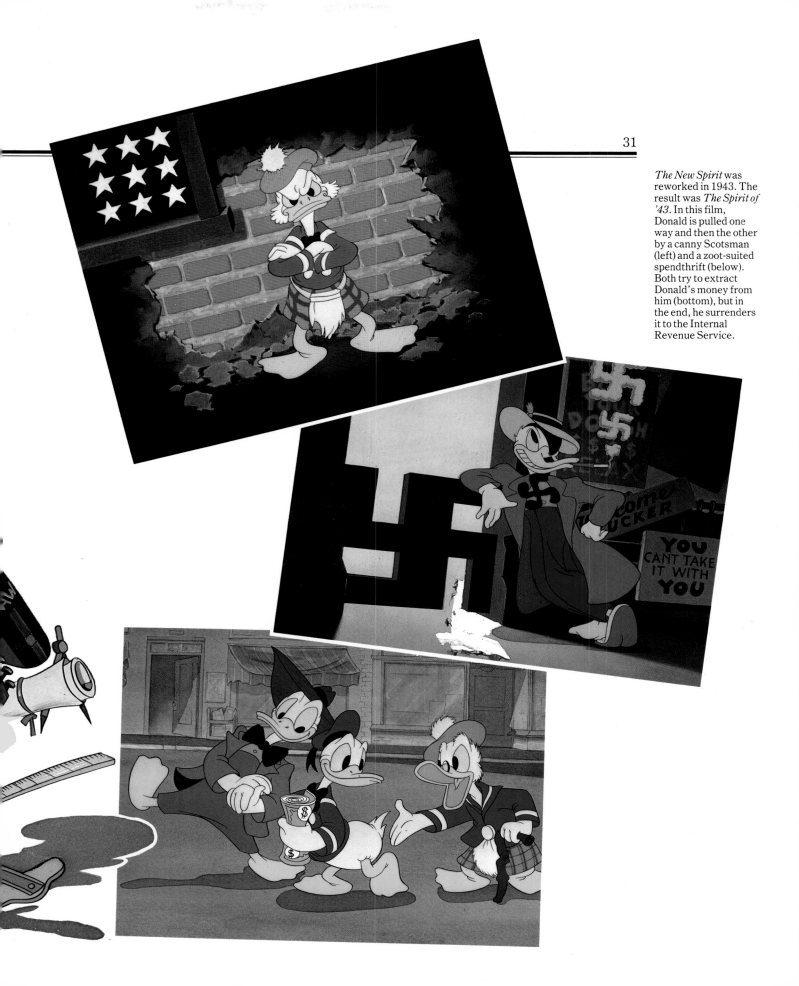

The New Spirit was reworked in 1943. The result was *The Spirit of '43*. In this film, Donald is pulled one way and then the other by a canny Scotsman (left) and a zoot-suited spendthrift (below). Both try to extract Donald's money from him (bottom), but in the end, he surrenders it to the Internal Revenue Service.

driven to madness by a rigid totalitarian state that allows little or no hope for the individual.

The film was to be called *Donald in Nutziland*, but its name was changed before release to the title of a song by Oliver Wallace that figures prominently in it. The song became a hit on the record charts. Donald is agonizingly effective, and the entire picture is an artistic *tour de force*. So powerful was its impact that it was translated and smuggled into Germany, much to the chagrin of the Nazi Party. Donald as symbol of the Allied struggle is beautifully captured by the film's poster, which has him pelting Hitler smack in the eye with a ripe tomato. The tomato's dripping remains are used in the film to form the letters of the words "The End."

The year 1943 also saw the release of *Flying Jalopy*, a "terriflying" attack on war profiteering, and *Home Defense*, in which Donald is abetted by the Nephews and malfunctions as a civilian aircraft spotter — by falling asleep.

The production of war shorts fell off in 1944. The Allies were more confident of a European victory, so they turned their attentions from the Nazis to the Pacific campaign. *Commando Duck* (1944) includes one of Disney's rare animated caricatures of a Japanese soldier who at one point quips "Japanese custom always shooting in back please." But Donald Duck war films never reached the level of chauvinism displayed by the vituperative Bugs Bunny or Popeye equivalents.

The Axis was very influential in Latin America during the war years and many of their propaganda films were circulated in theaters. The United States was worried about this influence, and sought to redress the balance through the Office of the Coordinator of Inter-American Affairs (CIAA), which was founded in 1940. The war had also closed

the European market, and America was seeking new commercial outlets abroad. So was Disney. 1941 had been financially disastrous for the Disney Studio whose distribution to 55 countries was now seriously curtailed.

As part of the "Good Neighbor" policy, the CIAA, with Nelson Rockefeller as its head, approached Disney with the offer of a goodwill tour of South America, where Disney was very popular. Disney agreed, stipulating that he would undertake a 2-month tour of Brazil, Argentina, Bolivia and Chile with a group of nine Studio artists on a non-

Both as soldier and citizen, Donald lent his support to the war effort. Cautionary posters, like the one shown below, appeared all over the United States. The posters were used by groups such as civilian aircraft spotters.

political basis. The objective would be to study the customs and culture of these exotic lands with a view to the production of several feature films.

"El Groupo," as they became known, left Los Angeles on August 17, 1941. The fruits of their mission included two feature films, *Saludos Amigos* (1943) and *The Three Caballeros* (1945), both highly successful and both allotting a prominent role to Donald Duck.

Donald was cast in both features as an irrepressible American tourist who is introduced to foreign scenes and customs by José Carioca, a dapper Brazilian parrot, and Panchito, a boisterous Mexican rooster. In both films, Donald functions as a goodwill ambassador, representing America in politically crucial areas. He also encourages his own countrymen to be open to foreign ideas,

ready and eager to learn and profit from new experiences, and to be good neighbors to their "Good Neighbor." That he was awarded such an important role was an indication of his popularity at home and abroad and an indication of his influence as an American archetype.

This merging of Donald's identity with that of national interests, both military and economic, is unique in screen annals. Perhaps it is best illustrated by the military insignia to which he lent his famous face. He was by far the most popular Disney mascot among war-time units and appeared on over 400 insignias. All the designs were supplied free of charge by Disney to the government.

Hundreds of military units adopted the feisty Duck as their mascot during the war. The many insignias that bore Donald's image indicated the extent of his popularity as a regimental symbol.

The Nephews have been the bane of their Unca Donald's existence ever since they arrived in his life in 1938. Left, below and bottom: These illustrations from 1938 show the Nephews in action.

In 1939, Gus Goose paid his cousin Donald a harrowing visit in *Donald's Cousin Gus*. Bottom left: Gus checks his unique timepiece and sees that the hand points to "Lunch."

One fateful day in 1938, Donald received a letter from his sister, Dumbella, who informed him of the imminent arrival of her three children (*Donald's Nephews*, 1938). Despite the numberless indignities Huey, Dewey and Louie have inflicted on their "Unca Donald" over the years, they have never left to go home. The obscure Dumbella seems not to have required them back, and it is not difficult to guess why.

Diabolical triplets, their angelic faces concealed a genius for terrorist plots, which were hatched, for the most part, with Donald as target. The Nephews could, and did, outwit their uncle, endanger his life and limbs and were a guaranteed impetus to raise his temper to the boiling point. Foils for the foil, they transformed Donald's life, thrusting him into unwitting parenthood and its contingent responsibilities. He was no longer an ageless duck. Suddenly the generation gap was in evidence, and it has proved fertile ground for disaster ever since.

The Nephews shared their looks as well as their sentences. But in the unending war with Donald, they have grown and developed, psychologically if not physically. They have proved themselves intelligent, resourceful, loyal, brave and even affectionate. Transcending their role as pint-sized hellions, they have become Donald's boon companions in adventure and adversity. Especially in the Carl Barks comics they are treated as super-children, spouting wit and wisdom beyond their years and rescuing their blundering uncle from catastrophes through superior mental faculties and exemplary moral courage. They even feel sorry for him and sometimes regret the trouble to which they have frequently but inadvertently put him.

Yet they remain children, engaging the admiration of younger readers who derive great satisfaction from the parent-child role reversal they personify. Not only do the Nephews get the better of Donald in domestic strife, but they are also better equipped to cope with life's dangers and disappointments. They are by comparison rational and not self-deceiving. Above all, they are free of Donald's compulsive need to prove himself.

The Nephews' origins are not the only shadowy area of duck genealogy that has been a source of contention for two generations of comics fanatics. Uncle Scrooge, for instance, is neither Grandma Duck's brother nor her son. And Grandma Duck *must* be at least 110 years old! The dubious Cousin Gus, who appeared in only one Donald short but ate his way through several comic strips, is a case in point. Billed as nephew of Luke the Goose, who married Donald's Aunt Daphne, sister to his father Quackmore, and therefore a distant cousin to Donald, Gus nevertheless proclaims himself dispatched by a mysterious Aunt Fanny. This spurious lineage is only a prelude to the even greater threat Gus poses to Donald's domestic security. The gluttonous goose proves to be an obsessive omnivore, and Donald is driven to fantastic lengths in the defense of his larder. The intruder sports a watch with hands that point only to Breakfast, Lunch and Dinner, the three appearing to merge into an endless orgy of consumption. Needless to say, Cousin Gus was not invited again.

Most of the Duck family began, like Gus, as bit players or foils for Donald. But Carl Barks populated Duckburg and reared a new supporting cast. Foremost among Donald's kin was the ever-popular Scrooge McDuck, described by Barks as "the richest old coot in

Uncle Scrooge McDuck, created by Carl Barks, became part of Donald's family in 1947. Below: The miserly millionaire Scrooge demonstrates his obsession with money.

the world.'' Scrooge appeared first in the comic book *Christmas on Bear Mountain* (1947) as a cantankerous miser with an aristocratic heritage as head of the Clan McDuck. He is drawn the same as Donald is, except for his sideburns and glasses, and his clothes, which are symbols of his established wealth. He wears a silk topper, frock coat, cane and spats. According to Barks, Scrooge is ''banker, industrialist, magnate and tycoon,'' master of three cubic acres of money, who knows the date on every dime of it. His stinginess is as notorious as his wealth. He places Donald in the same demeaning positions as Donald does his Nephews, but with greater success. Not only does Scrooge employ all four, forcing them to maintain and guard his mountains of gold, but he also leads them on fantastic adventures in quest of even greater wealth. He

is an old Shylock, pouring over his ledgers, begrudging Donald a dime for coffee and buying a restaurant for a million dollars rather than pay his nephew's check for $9.75.

Donald's true nemesis, however, was his cousin, Gladstone Gander. This arrogant, wavy-haired dandy and con-man was described by Barks as ''loafer, bum, chiseler and connoisseur of the fast buck.'' He represents the obsession with luck, as does Scrooge the obsession with money, and he is the focus of Donald's deepest resentments. Gladstone scorns work and regards himself as Donald's intellectual superior. He is, in fact, a perversion of Donald's original nature,

Right: Grandma Duck was the upholder of morality in Donald's life. She was created in 1943.

Below: Gyro Gearloose, the nutty inventor chicken, was created by Carl Barks in 1952.

GRANDMA'S BILL IS SHORTER THAN DONALD'S

AVOID SPRADDLE-LEGGED POSES

recalling Donald's early behavior in *The Wise Little Hen* (1934) when he was the hedonistic vice president of the Idle Hour Club.

An antidote to Gladstone's supine self-assurance — "All things come to him who sits and waits" — and its corrupting influence on Donald, is Grandma Duck, who appeared in the comic strips in 1943. With her Victorian hairstyle, leg-of-mutton sleeves and high-buttoned boots, she embodies sturdy, old-fashioned virtues. A strict disciplinarian, she exhorts her family to work and disapproves of frivolity in all forms, especially in Daisy!

Like Cousin Gus, this guardian of morals tended to pay disconcerting visits. Grandma is still used often in new foreign comic material, much of which is originated by the Studio, but not published in the USA.

Gyro Gearloose, another of Barks' crackpot characters, made his comic debut in 1952. An inventor chicken, certifiably mad, but sometimes a genius, Gyro represents another special ability which Donald lacks — technical knowledge. With Gyro, however, technology becomes an end in itself, and he creates wondrous devices that are of little or no practical use. Numbered among his achievements are a jet-powered baggage buggy that runs on a quart of fire crackers, trained worms and a hydraulic peanut-butter spreader.

Donald's other uncle, Ludwig von Drake, is a more recent upstart, developed in 1961 purely for television. He is the archetypal dotty professor with an Austrian accent, expert on everything and willing to dip into his vast fund of knowledge at the least provocation. He delivered a popular series of lectures for the television show, *Walt Disney's Wonderful World of Color*, during the 1960s and became a comic strip figure in 1961 following his television debut.

Below: A family gathering. Gladstone Gander, Donald's arrogant cousin, meets with Ludwig von Drake, Donald's dotty professor uncle.

Right: Donald at the ready! The Duck attempts to save his good pal Mickey from disaster in *Alpine Climbers* (1936).

Below: Donald's early gang of chums included Pluto, Horace Horsecollar and Clarabelle Cow.

The true extent of Donald's family has only emerged over the decades, but most of his friends and acquaintances have been with him from the very beginning. He was originally part of a group of characters who appeared in both the film and comic strip versions of the *Silly Symphonies* — barnyard chums cavorting amid rural settings. In the Disney books of the 1930s, as well as the strips and films, Donald interacted with the entire group — Mickey Mouse, Minnie, Goofy, Mickey's nephews, Clarabelle Cow and Horace Horsecollar. The latter two did not long survive the move to films. Even the gifted Clara Cluck of *Orphan's Benefit* fame did not thrive in the cinema.

As a rising film star, Donald played opposite Mickey, Pluto and Goofy in a series of Mickey Mouse shorts. Though he had attained top billing in his own series by 1937, he also continued to appear in Mickey Mouse cartoons, which brings us to the unavoidable issue of the friendly rivalry between Donald Duck and Mickey Mouse.

Originally cast as an *agent provocateur* for Mickey, Donald's popularity rapidly rose to equal that of the Mouse. Donald's aggressive personality was an immediate sensation. Before his advent, audiences were used to decorous, happy-go-lucky chicks and rabbits whose personas, compared with Donald's, were fairly nebulous. Among these early stars, Mickey reigned supreme.

Disney himself originally did Mickey's voice, and the Mouse was said to reflect many aspects of Disney's own character. In fact, artists and story men kept him in mind when working on the Mouse. Walt was the soul of Mickey, yet he recognized his creation's comic limitations. "Donald Duck is an escape, a relief from Mickey's inhibitions. He is a very outrageous fellow, with bad manners and a worse temper, and every-

Below: Dainty Minnie Mouse meets up with Goofy. Donald, Mickey and Goofy appeared together in numerous Mickey Mouse cartoons between 1935 and 1942.

The best of friends and friendly rivals. Donald served as a foil for Mickey in the shorts of the mid-1930s. Below: Here are the pals in *Mickey's Amateurs* (1937).

one is very fond of him, including myself,'' Disney commented in 1936.

The truth was that Mickey was a bit too good. Ever cheerful, he was not capable of the strong outbursts that were possible with the Duck. Mickey was an equable creature with an ego well under control. He had no dark side to his nature. He wasn't paradoxical and therefore lacked flexibility. He had gone from little hero to straight man. By the time Donald made his entrance, Mickey was more than ready for a foil.

Mickey had come to represent the forces of order and sanity as opposed to the subversive anarchy of Donald. Their antithetical relationship is epitomized in *The Band Concert* (1935), in which

Mickey's noble efforts to uphold culture and decorum are undermined by the raucous Duck. Supremely expressive as he is, Mickey is no match for Donald's iconoclasm. The film works well — Toscanini saw it six times — because the two heroes are so beautifully contrasted. Mickey represents what we *should* be, and Donald what we *are*.

Said Jack Hannah, ''Many times I saw it happen where they would start out a picture with Mickey in mind, and pretty soon the story took on a little twist, and they'd start getting a little rougher with the character and it seemed like the gags got a little broader. Immediately we found that for Mickey — it didn't fit him. And somebody would say, 'Now you're getting into the Duck's character!' The main reason was that Mickey was a little hero type, and there weren't too many scripts that would fit that.''

Donald's family and friends meet up once more in this nostalgic painting by Carl Barks. Entitled "*A 1934 Belchfire Runabout!*," the work is Barks' 50th-birthday tribute to Donald. A limited edition lithograph of the painting has been released by Another Rainbow Publishing. See also page 81.

Pierre (Bad Pete) in pursuit! Over the years, this arch-fiend has menaced not only Donald but also Mickey and other Disney stars. Below: In this still from *Timber* (1941), Donald is on his own after Pierre has pulled the Duck's railroad handcar apart.

Donald's capacity for frustration was such that not even his family or friends could fill the "aggravation gap." So Disney story men contrived a string of adversaries for him, which ranged in size from a bee to a bear.

In *Modern Inventions* (1937), Donald was pitted against an array of gadgets, including a robot. Over the years he has been provoked by a variety of other inanimate objects including automobiles, airplanes and rubber hoses. All seem to possess a will of their own and to have been invented with the sole purpose of driving him to frenzy.

Then there are the animate antagonists — Bad Pete, formerly Peg Leg Pete, who has lurked around since the early Mickey days; Barks' villainous Beagle Boys, intent on spiriting away Scrooge's hard-earned cash; and Donald's next-door neighbors, the Joneses, a less-virulent strain of the human species. Humphrey the Bear has wreaked havoc in his wilderness setting, and, in Bolivia, Donald had to contend with a whimsical, recalcitrant llama. He has also numbered a gorilla among his many combatants.

But the Duck lends himself particularly to torment by small creatures, as by a bee in *Bee at the Beach* (1950) and by ants in *Tea for Two Hundred* (1948). Among these agents of mischief none can surpass the chipmunks, Chip and Dale, for troublesome antics. Introduced by Jack Hannah in 1947, the chipmunks were a huge success with audiences and never failed to keep Donald on the hop. He is constantly thwarted by their machinations. Over the years, they have proved themselves spoilers of even the best-laid plans of mice and ducks and paragons of minimenace.

Far left: Outnumbered, outsmarted and undone by a band of thieving chipmunks, Donald gets tangled up in a folding camp chair. The chipmunks get a free picnic in this still from *Donald's Vacation* (1940).

In *Modern Inventions* (1937), Donald was pitted against an array of inanimate adversaries, including the robot shown on the left.

Humphrey the Bear proved a formidable antagonist for Donald in films such as *Grin and Bear It* (1954), *Bearly Asleep* (1955) and *Beezy Bear* (1955). Below: Humphrey creeps up on Donald in the film poster for *Grin and Bear It*.

Romance comes to us all. Suddenly in 1937 it blossomed in the life of D. Duck Esq. The film *Don Donald* found him in a Latin American setting. Astride a donkey and sporting a sombrero, Donald's heart was set aflame by a fiery señorita named Donna Duck. This mantilla-ed *chiquita*, with languishing lashes and a mean left hook, was the embodiment of all the female vices. She was vain, capricious and devoid of humor or gratitude. When Donald's car broke down, she whipped a unicycle from her purse and pedaled out of his life without a backward glance.

Donald wooed Donna with infinite pains and minimal gratification, but she played an important part in his individualization. In 1937, Webb Smith of the Disney Story Department said, "We have a chance to show Donald in moods we have never shown in any other picture. We have always had him squawking — we never had a chance to make an actor of him!"

But it was another three years before this world of emotion was truly opened to Donald. In *Mr. Duck Steps Out* (1940),

Donna reappeared, modified in apparel if not temper. She was still the vivacious flirt who could wrap Donald around her dainty little finger, but she now sported a puffy sleeved blouse, Minnie Mouse shoes and a perky pink bow. Her eyelashes were kept, and put to very effective use. Donna had gone from woman of mystery to archetypal girlfriend — enter Daisy Duck.

Ducky Nash did Daisy's voice until the 1950s when the Studio attempted to make her more appealing by substituting voices of various women in the Inking Department. In spite of these innovations, Daisy never developed as Donald did. A beguiling voice was not sufficient to rescue her from the role of perpetual girlfriend, and she tended to remain a one-dimensional personality, orbiting around Donald as his female counterpart. She was not even allowed to become his wife, and they have never shared

Don meets Donna and the feathers fly. The captivating Señorita Donna Duck was Donald's first love, but she only appeared as Donna in *Don Donald* (1937).

Left: Donna became Daisy, the woman in Donald's life, in 1940 in *Mr. Duck Steps Out*. Daisy went on to make a new man of Donald.

Below: Dapper Donald, armed with flowers and chocolates, arrives to court Daisy in *Crazy Over Daisy* (1950).

domestic "blitz." Moreover, she is almost the only woman in an environment populated almost exclusively by males. Life must get lonely.

Still, Daisy has had her moments. In *Cured Duck* (1945) she went to great lengths to make a better man of Donald. She even insisted that he learn to control his temper. She drove him to a jealous frenzy in *Donald's Double Trouble* (1946). But her ultimate performance was surely

Right: In this still from *Cured Duck* (1945), Daisy sprays herself with her favorite perfume as she prepares for a date with Donald. She was the archetypal girlfriend — coquettish, vain and generally pretty difficult to please.

Below: In *Donald's Double Trouble* (1946), Donald uses all the charm he possesses to win back Daisy.

in the 1947 short, *Donald's Dilemma*. Accidentally hit on the head by a flowerpot, Donald loses his memory and his usual voice and begins to croon "à la Crosby." An overnight sensation, he finds himself the idol of millions, and he wants nothing further to do with poor Daisy. Distraught, she consults a psychiatrist who regards her as no better than a duck in the manger. The psychiatrist asks her to whom she thinks Donald ought to belong, herself or the world. Without any hesitation whatsoever she shrieks "Me! Me! Me!"

Daisy really established her presence in the early comic strips, first appearing as Donald's new neighbor. During the 1950s, she began to bear a striking resemblance to the wives and girlfriends in contemporary television sitcoms. She was basically scatter-brained, a terrible driver and golfer, addicted to silly hats and so on. This was the tiresome repertoire of feeble, female gags made at the female's expense. In those years Daisy was petty, irrational, quarrelsome and continually scheming for Donald's attention. She was not above resorting to verbal and physical abuse.

Barks seldom used her in his comic books, treating her more as an emblem than a personality. He filled her bill with memorably weak lines such as "Giggle, giggle!" In Barks' world, she is something to be appeased, placated and fought for, a prize to be won, with Gladstone as well as Donald often competing for her favors. She is a creature of ritual with a yen for presents and pearls — *real* pearls. Her temper has degenerated, and she is chronically late for appointments.

Yes, Daisy has been much maligned. Perhaps Disney's initial assumption was that given the sort of fellow Donald was, how could he be expected to consort with anyone *but* the wrong woman? He needed a provocation, not a person, someone guaranteed to make a sap out of him. Daisy provided yet a further opportunity for Donald to play "true to form," although she has often done her best to make a worthy man of him. Moreover, she has been given little opportunity to display what may be a trove of hidden virtues.

One virtue cannot be denied her. Despite the batting of the odd eyelash, Daisy has proved herself true blue. And her loyalty to Donald must be considered beyond question. It has been said that, similar to Della Street, she'll wait until the seas dry up. For 46 years she has maintained a relationship that can hardly be called well-defined or replete with prospects. Hope of a firmer arrangement must long since have faded. Donald is a difficult Duck, but she *must* love him. She has shown herself to be not only a very good friend, but a woman of independence, able to love and let love.

So, is Daisy a feather-brain, a mere catalyst for Donald's antics or a more-liberated woman than we know? The question remains unanswered.

On one occasion, the tables were turned and Daisy did the pleading. In *Donald's Dilemma* (1947), Daisy clings to Donald in an effort to persuade him to give up his new-found fame and glory as the crooning idol of millions.

DONALD COMES TO LIFE

ANIMATING DONALD

Donald made his appearance at a critical moment. Disney had forged rapidly into uncharted territory, and by 1933 his animators had mastered the basics of their art. Unencumbered by endless detail and an enormous assembly-line operation, artists were free to lay the foundations for all future work in the cartoon field. Donald's career grew with theirs, for he emerged and flourished during animation's "High Renaissance" from 1935 to 1943.

During this period, Disney strove beyond the limitations of the medium, trying to make the cartoon more than a string of gimmicks and gags. He sought to build comedy through an understanding of the feelings of characters. He stressed the importance of personality in his animal stars. He encouraged artists to strike a balance between realism and exaggeration, and achieve the caricature of realism that obsessed him. On the one hand, animators were encouraged to work in a rough, free style. "Rough drawings open the way to stronger action. The animator feels the movement with his whole body and transfers this intensity to the character," said Frank Thomas and Ollie Johnston in *Disney Animation — The Illusion of Life*. Donald lent himself perfectly to this style. Simultaneously, Disney stressed the importance of detail. He wanted a sense of weight, accurate anatomy and the sort of "follow through" that gives fluidity and a clear line to the action.

He instituted art classes for the animators, and they drew from live models. In the open, exploratory atmosphere of the Studio, animators were able to learn from each other. The fruits of their collective achievements were codified and used to train new generations of animators. Said Les Clark, "Today it may look simple to us. At the time it wasn't. It was something that hadn't been tried before or proved." Under Disney's guidance, artists gradually isolated, named and classified the techniques they had discovered through accident or education.

Such standard principles as "Straight Ahead" or "Pose to Pose" action, "Squash and Stretch" and "Anticipation" grew directly out of this experimentation. Head animators made model sheets for their characters and for the drawing of various emotions. They developed types of action — cycle, repeat action, crossover, ripple and so forth. The quest for new and better methods was unending. According to Frank Thomas and Ollie Johnston, Disney stressed the necessity for "getting animators into the spirit of the picture and not making them feel outsiders just executing something worked out by someone else." When asked by an employee of another studio what it was that made Disney films superior, one animator replied, "We analyze."

The collaborative, additive process included a freedom to develop individually. Disney artists were young men,

Far left: One of the numerous story board sketches for *Donald's Nephews*, the 1938 short in which Huey, Dewey and Louie made their first appearance.

Left: Donald tries to control his annoyance with the "tick-tock" of a huge clock in this fine animator's sketch for *Clock Cleaners* (1937). In the film, Donald, Mickey and Goofy are hired to clean an enormous clock on the side of a skyscraper.

finding themselves as well as their craft. Imaginations ran wild while they worked like Trojans. Ward Kimball, one of Disney's finest animators, described the atmosphere. "We thought we were always going to be 21 years old. We thought we would always be putting goldfish in the bottled drinking water, balancing cups of water on the light fixtures, changing the labels on cans of sauerkraut juice. We were 21 years old, Walt was 30, leading the pack. Working there was more fun than any job I could ever imagine."

The cross-pollination and *esprit de corps* are best reflected in the phenomenon of the story board. Credited to Webb Smith, it was perhaps this innovation more than any other that gave Disney films their firm structure and plot line. It became the crucial component of the preproduction process.

It was the function of the Story Department to generate ideas. The Layout Department would then stage the scenes and transfer instructions to the animators. Though there was a story research man, the actual origins of a story are often elusive. "A picture is not started upon in the Disney Studio," wrote Robert D. Feild in *The Art of Walt Disney*. "It happens into being by fortuitous circumstance. It evolves as a result of interplay between the happy accident and intense concentration. As a result of the free cooperation of minds, ideas are in constant circulation...always being improved upon."

A cartoon had no script, so the story men projected their ideas directly by means of pictographs. These were often no more than scribbled sketches, the sudden crystallization of an idea which leaped from mind to paper — an arrested gesture, a captured bit of time. The rough drawings were pinned to boards that were hung on all available wall space. About 60 to 70 sketches could be attached to each board, which measured 7×5ft (2.1×1.5m).

Story men were not concerned with how well the sketches were drawn, but whether or not they conveyed an idea or emotion. Pictures had to have an immediate impact or they were thrown away. It was the pattern that mattered, not the details. Yet the sketches from the early years constitute some of the most inspired art of the Disney Studio, in a sense, its "fine art." There are thousands of such drawings in the Walt Disney Archives, mostly anonymous, though closer inspection reveals individual styles. The interest, beauty and power of these roughs have been appreciated only recently. They are literally pictures of brainstorms, and they look it. Absolutely free and unconstrained, their frenzied mobility reflects not only the speed at which the men were working but their absolute sureness of touch. Consequently, the roughs have a vitality and gutsiness that are absent in the smooth refinement of the finished art work.

Unlike other studios, where everyone worked in isolation and guarded their secrets, Disney artists were continually showing and sharing their accomplishments and mistakes. They formed a kind of collective genius,

Below and bottom right: Two details from a model sheet for *Donald's Golf Game* (1938) show Donald and the Nephews impeccably attired in golfing outfits. This model sheet provided animators with reference to comparative sizes of the cartoon's characters and their golf clubs.

controlled and stimulated by Disney himself. The Story Department was arranged so artists could borrow from one another all the time.

When working on a drawing or story idea, story men attempted to project themselves intensely into their creations. The artist actually became Donald or Mickey. They acted out gestures or poses for each other, using mirrors, dressing up, pulling grotesque faces, resorting to props. They helped each other get inside their characters.

There was no rigid production schedule, though each of them might have been involved in up to six films simultaneously. They tried numerous working methods and found that, in the Story Department particularly, a team procedure succeeded best. Once the initial story research had been done, the director would gather his staff, explain all he knew about the story so far, then split his men into groups of two or three. Each group was responsible for working out a separate sequence. Director Jack Hannah described how he and Carl Barks worked together when they were both story men before the war.

"Carl and I closed the door and, just horsing around, we'd get to talking back and forth and maybe the suggestion of a locale would start it off. It might be a circus, Donald Duck late for school, as a kid, a dream he had, it didn't matter. So we'd just toss this around between us. Usually with no one else. Other times an idea came from a book or was suggested by somebody else. But usually it was started — 'given birth' — by just a suggestion or a thought. We'd hash it over. Carl

Disney artists went to great lengths to grasp the personalities of their animal creations. It was common practice for story men to mime postures, gestures and reactions for one another. Left: This 1937 photograph shows Harry Reeves, head of the Story Department at that time, getting into the mood of *Good Scouts*.

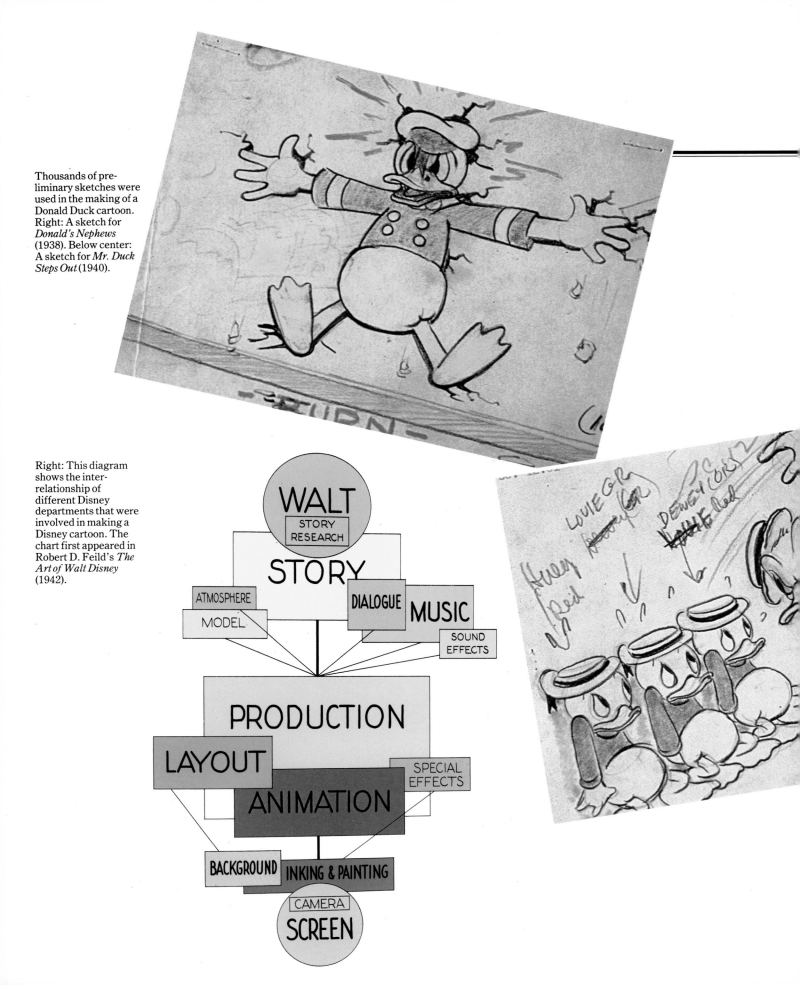

Thousands of pre-liminary sketches were used in the making of a Donald Duck cartoon. Right: A sketch for *Donald's Nephews* (1938). Below center: A sketch for *Mr. Duck Steps Out* (1940).

Right: This diagram shows the inter-relationship of different Disney departments that were involved in making a Disney cartoon. The chart first appeared in Robert D. Feild's *The Art of Walt Disney* (1942).

would build up a certain little idea, and then I would maybe put a top on that or suggest a different direction and that would influence his thinking and pretty soon we got something going and when it began to sound interesting we'd stop. He'd take a section and I'd take a section, and we'd go to our desks right in the same room and rough sketch — story sketch — and then start blocking it out on the board, and then build it from there."

When they reached a point where feedback was required, they told the head of the department they were ready for a meeting. "Other crews would come and we'd have a rap session and they'd throw off gags and usually the director would come in" said Hannah. "It would be our discretion as to whether we used their gags, and sometimes a whole new situation or a whole new trend of the story would come up through the ideas of the different men." When they felt they "had it," Walt would come in, and they would show him the boards, telling the story sketch by sketch.

Directors and story men tended to follow through with one character, and directors built around them a team of animators who specialized in that character. Many found that they could not deal with Donald. But men like Hannah, Barks and King related to his zany personality, as did his first animators, Art Babbitt and Dick Huemer, and story man Roy Williams. Dick Lundy, Fred Spencer and Harry Reeves were also Duck Men and worked mainly on his pictures. There was also a finer level of specialization within the Duck

Left: A fresh, free animator's drawing for the 1938 short, *Donald's Better Self*.

unit. Some animators were better on Donald's broader, more raucous aspects, while others could evoke whimsy or tenderness. Like actors, they identified with certain roles and characteristics.

With growth and success, the Disney Studio became more complex and intricate. New departments were established, highly specialized, yet constantly interacting. By the 1940s, the Disney hierarchy was producing Donald Duck cartoons, among other shorts and features, at the rate of seven to eight a year. The procedure for making a film, once it had progressed beyond the pre-production stage of the story board into full production, illustrates the complexities of the medium and the skill of those who worked with it.

When the story research was complete, the story board was given to the director who, together with the Sound Department, computed the mathematics of the sound track. The total time of the film, for example an 8-minute short, would determine the length of footage required. This was subdivided according to the number of scenes. The time for each scene was calculated very precisely so that when the director handed out work sheets to animators, they knew exactly how much footage they would have to draw, as well as what the action and sound would be in each scene.

The sound track was then recorded. Three separate tracks were made — for dialogue, sound effects and music. A "bar sheet" was used to coordinate music and animation. To this point, no animation at all would have been done, but

when action and sound were brought together for the first time, they *always* matched perfectly.

Following instructions from the Sound Department, head animators drew the extremes of movement in a sequence. Head animators prepared the crucial points of the action, such as one, eight and sixteen in a series of sixteen frames, while the so-called "in-betweeners" filled in the gaps. The animators' rough sketches were then photographed and projected similar to a slide show. Disney always saw this pencil test, along with staff from the various departments, usually younger people such as inkers, painters and in-betweeners who were not working on the picture. Their audible reactions were considered very important, and they were also given questionnaires about their response to the film. Afterward, everyone met in the hall where Disney made his assessment, either a go-ahead or an okay with changes.

The animators' rough sketches were $9\frac{1}{2} \times 12\frac{1}{2}$in (24 × 31.7cm). These were given to the clean up men who refined them to a single line. Inking and painting came next. This was the only operation performed exclusively by women whose smaller hands were more suited to the delicate work. They transferred the final art work in ink onto clear celluloid sheets known as "cels." In the 1950s, this step was replaced by an adaptation of the Xerox process developed by Ub Iwerks, one of Disney's earliest animators. Color, in tones determined by the Color Model Department, was then applied to the reverse side of the cel. Finally, the Camera Department positioned the characters against previously painted backgrounds and photographed them onto the film strip, each exposure made separately by means of stop-action photography.

Until the 1950s, inking and painting were processes done exclusively by women. Top left: In this photograph, an inker works on a cel for *The Three Caballeros* (1945). Note the use of cotton mittens to prevent hand moisture getting onto the cel.

Bottom left: Donald — whistle at the ready — and one of the Nephews step out of a model sheet for *Good Scouts* (1938).

The Wise Little Hen was Disney's 45th *Silly Symphony* but only the 17th cartoon in color. Donald's screen debut in this 1934 film marked an appearance in color even before Mickey Mouse. The film deals with the efforts of the thrifty Wise Little Hen to enlist the help of her loutish neighbors, Donald Duck and Peter Pig, in sowing and reaping her corn. Donald complains of a stomachache but makes a miraculous recovery when the time comes to dine on her hot corn bread. Mrs Hen administers his "just deserts" in the form of a spoonful of castor oil. Despite these inauspicious beginnings in an obscure rural setting, Donald's anti-heroics caused an immediate sensation. He became the first *Silly Symphony* character to be featured in a Mickey Mouse cartoon.

In *Orphan's Benefit*, also made in 1934, Donald threw his initial tantrum, squawked and flapped uproariously. Above all, he exhibited a dogged persis-tence that established the basis of his character. Heckled and jeered at by the merciless orphans, all mice, he is pelted with bricks and flowerpots and eventually jerked off the stage. But each new humiliation only fires his resolution. He stubbornly perseveres with his recitations, and nothing can force him to surrender the stage — a truly remarkable performance.

Donald was immediately cast again as the antagonist for *The Band Concert* (1935). This classic short was the first Mickey Mouse cartoon in color. It pits Donald, as a peanut and ice cream vendor with musical predilections, against the earnest, dedicated concert master, Mickey. Once again, Donald goes to any lengths to secure the limelight and succeeds in undermining Mickey's performance of *William Tell* by repeatedly playing *Turkey in the Straw* on the piccolo. The result is pandemonium.

Donald's first film appearance was in the 1934 *Silly Symphony*, *The Wise Little Hen*. Right: The little hen with her loutish neighbors, Donald Duck and Peter Pig. Center: A leaky house-boat was Donald's home in the film.

Orphan's Benefit was the second cartoon in which Donald appeared. The film was originally released in black-and-white in 1934. A color remake came out in 1941. Far right: The film poster for the later version.

Left: Mickey calls the shots in *Magician Mickey*. Donald, still the heckler, gets his "come-uppance" in this Mickey Mouse cartoon of 1937.

An enduring friendship. Below: Mickey and Donald together again in the 1983 featurette, *Mickey's Christmas Carol*—49 years after their first performance together in *Orphan's Benefit*.

Audiences and critics loved it, and Donald won national acclaim. Critics wrote, "Never in motion pictures has there been such a funny fury as Donald's." "The greatest pest since chain letters."

From 1935 to 1942, Donald co-starred in 26 Mickey cartoons, including *Mickey's Service Station* and *Mickey's Fire Brigade* in 1935, *Alpine Climbers* and *Mickey's Circus* in 1936, and *Hawaiian Holiday, Magician Mickey, Clock Cleaners* and *Lonesome Ghosts*, all in 1937. Most of the Mickey series were trio films featuring Donald, Mickey and Goofy. These shorts are considered by many to be the best cartoons ever to come out of the Disney Studio. The standard format has the three friends approaching a given situation, splitting up for solo episodes, then regrouping for the finale. The popularity of these shorts began to wane by the end of the 1930s, and Mickey's *Symphony Hour* of 1942 was Donald's last appearance in a Mickey Mouse cartoon for 41 years. But 1947 saw the trio together again for the "Mickey and the Beanstalk" sequence of *Fun and Fancy Free*, one of the few features to co-star Donald, Mickey and Goofy. To add to its charm, it had a narration by Edgar Bergen and Charlie McCarthy.

In 1937, Donald became the Studio's first character since Mickey to have his own cartoon series. *Don Donald* cast him as an improbable Latin lover. He was without the support of any of the Disney stable of stars, but was accompanied by Daisy's prototype, the infamous Donna Duck. *Modern Inventions* was also released in 1937. Again, Donald was alone, but this time amid a terrifying assortment of machinery run amuck. Between 1938 and 1942, he appeared in seven or eight Donald Duck cartoons a

Left: Donald's performance in *Der Fuehrer's Face* received wide acclaim. His 1943 "nightmare in Nutziland" won the Studio an Academy Award.

Below: The intrepid trio, Mickey, Goofy and Donald, take on the inhabitants of a haunted house in the classic short, *Lonesome Ghosts* (1937).

Right: His nation's "eyes and ears," Donald is an enthusiastic tourist amid Bolivia's dramatic scenery in the first of Disney's Latin American features, *Saludos Amigos* (1943).

Center: In Disney's second Latin American feature, *The Three Caballeros* (1945), Donald, Panchito and José Carioca indulge in high kicks and high spirits.

The three "caballeros" shoot, dance and generally live it up in one of the most famous Disney animation sequences in *The Three Caballeros* (1945).

year. And he was gathering his own cinematic entourage. The Nephews arrived in 1938 and Donna became Daisy in 1940. This series of shorts included many of his "job" roles — Donald the problem-solver wreaking havoc in a variety of occupations as in *Officer Duck* (1939), *The Riveter* (1940), *Donald's Dog Laundry* (1940), *Window Cleaners* (1940) and *Truant Officer Donald* (1941).

The war years were devoted to patriotic roles. The most famous was *Der Fuehrer's Face*, which won an Academy Award. See *Donald the Patriot*, pages 28 to 33. During this period, Donald was also a major participant in Disney's 1941 Latin America venture which produced the two feature films, *Saludos Amigos* and *The Three Caballeros. Lake Titicaca*, taken from *Saludos Amigos*, was also released as a short. In the latter film Donald plays the naive but enthusiastic tourist who is introduced to Latin America by José Carioca, a Brazilian parrot and Panchito, a Mexican rooster. They are the "Three Caballeros" of the title, cavorting in exotic settings in glorious Technicolor and dancing intoxicating sambas with human señoritas.

These two films launched a new era for Disney in which the Studio moved more toward live action. Until that time, no attempt had been made to mix cartoon technique with live action since the 1920s when Disney experimented with the medium in his *Alice Comedies*.

The Latin American films demonstrate how sophisticated the Studio had become. *The Three Caballeros* was billed by the Studio as "the most startling advance in motion picture technique since the advent of sound," and it provoked almost as much controversy as *Fantasia*. No one had seen anything like it. It is one of the most imaginative pieces of animation ever produced by the Disney Studio. The use of color surpasses anything in both boldness and range. The exciting syncopation of music and movement is irresistible as the three pals scramble over each other. A famous dance scene shows Donald, José and Panchito wildly pursuing Aurora Miranda and other Brazilian beauties against an increasingly surrealistic background. Donald's unbridled libido led one writer to dub him a "web-footed wolf." Though critical reaction was originally mixed, the film has been well received in recent years. Said critic Leonard Maltin in 1973, "It was years ahead of its time in conception and execution."

During the 1940s and 1950s, the Disney team produced an 8-minute short every three weeks, in addition to feature films. The period was a heyday for Donald. *Working for Peanuts* (1953), with Chip and Dale, was his first three-dimensional cartoon. In 1954 and 1955, he appeared in Jack Hannah's famous forest ranger series with Humphrey the Bear in *Grin and Bear It* and *Beezy Bear*. A series of "how-to" educational films was released between 1956 and 1961. These films included *How to Have an Accident at Work* and *Donald and the Wheel*. The most outstanding was *Donald in Mathmagic Land* in which Donald explores the mysteries of numbers. This featurette is regarded as one of the most successful educational films ever made.

The mid-1950s saw a shift in tastes, and theaters began to show double bills rather than cartoons and selected short subjects. The 8-minute cartoon went the way of the newsreel, and Disney could no longer justify spending $75,000 on a short. The Studio stopped making cartoons altogether, and Disney phased out his short-subject units, laying off some staff and reassigning others to the Disneyland television programs. Donald's appearances on television were numerous, but he made no more cartoons. His last was *The Litterbug*, released in 1961.

Donald's classic shorts have been rereleased on American pay television channels and he has recently appeared in the 1983 featurette, *Mickey's Christmas Carol*. In this film he is cast out of his more-usual character as the mild-mannered nephew of Scrooge.

In many of his films, Donald proved he could be instructive as well as entertaining. His "educational" cartoons included *How to Have an Accident at Work* (left) and *Donald in Mathmagic Land* (bottom left). Both films were released in 1959.

From innovative private to pilot extraordinaire — is there nothing this Duck can't do? Left: The film poster for the 1942 short, *The Vanishing Private.* Center: A still from the 1943 short, *Flying Jalopy*, in which Donald urges on his rickety old plane in an effort to escape the flames behind him.

DONALD IN PRINT

DUCK BOOKS

The Adventures of Mickey Mouse was one of the first Disney story books. Printed in full color, it was published in 1931 by David McKay of New York and sold for 50 cents. This book, which continued to be reprinted until World War II, is especially interesting because mention is made in it of a Donald Duck. "This story," the text reads, "is about Mickey Mouse, who lives in a cozy nest under the floor of the old barn...Mickey has many friends in the old barn and barnyard. There are Henry Horse and Carolyn Cow and Patricia Pig and Donald Duck." A Donald Duck is also referred to and drawn in a book that was published in London around 1932 by Dean & Son. The strange bird depicted in this volume bears only the faintest resemblance to the Donald of later years. These are the earliest two book references to any Disney duck character.

It was not until 1935, after his screen debut the year before in The Wise Little Hen, that Donald appeared in a book of his own. Donald Duck was 14 pages long and published by Whitman Publishing of Racine, Wisconsin. This story concerned Donald's misadventures at a swimming hole with Mickey's two nephews, who bore a strong resemblance to the mouse audience of Orphan's Benefit (1934). Neither of the mice had names, but they referred to Donald as "Uncle." 1935 also saw the publication by McKay of The Wise Little Hen story. In 1936, a book

The covers of two of the earliest books in which Donald was featured. The Wise Little Hen was published by McKay in 1935, hard on the heels of the film's release in 1934. The very first Donald Duck book (right) was published by Whitman in 1935. It was 14 pages long and printed on linen-like paper.

ORE 'HOOZOO'

m and Dick and Harry Bun
ugh at Mickey with a gun,
owing they are safe and sound,
-key couldn't hit the ground.

onald Duck and Clara Hen,
bert Rooster, Jenny Wren,
ickey's many farmyard
                 friends.
They'll not catch him when
                 he bends.

a Owl if she'd a chance
 would lead our
 friend a
  pretty
  dance.

A Donald prototype?
The peculiar bird in
the lower left-hand
corner of this
illustration is referred
to as Donald Duck.
The picture comes
from an early *Mickey
Mouse Annual*,
published around 1932
by the English firm,
Dean & Son.

donald duck

Story written and illustrated by the staff of
the Walt Disney Studios.

B...

...ssion, Donald...
...wimming ch...
...so fine...
...Mous...

Mickey's nephews clapped their hands in glee.
They told Donald that they would meet him at
the swimming pool, and off they skipped down
the path, laughing and shouting.

? Who says I can't swim?" quacked
"All my family are champion
...the champion of my family!
...get my swimming suit!"

Nephews have always been a source of aggravation for Donald. This time, it is Mickey's mischievous nephews who lure Donald to disaster at the old swimming hole. Whitman published this first Donald Duck book in 1935. The book's title page and a selection of story pages are shown here.

Then the nephews lay on their
water hiding everything but t
toes. They looked as if fl
"Show us how to dive, D

With a big spring, Donald bounced high into the air. Then down he came, head first, his nose pointing right for the water and the splash. But instead of a splash there was a SCRUNCH!

When Donald finally freed his head, he stood up. He was very angry. "What's the matter, Uncle Donald?" Mickey's nephews asked innocently. "Oh, oy!" quacked Donald. "That water's HARD!"

entitled *Donald Duck*, that sold for 50 cents, was also published.

In all these volumes, Donald still lived on a houseboat and was very much the cranky idler of his first film. Visually he was the preclassic Donald, with a long bill, plump body, knobby knees and undefined hands. The first publications became bestsellers. Not surprisingly, Donald was quickly snapped up by other publishers, including the American firms of Dell, Simon & Schuster, Heath & Co, Random House and Grosset & Dunlap.

Donald Duck appeared in Mickey Mouse books and in the *Mickey Mouse Annual*. In 1947, Simon & Schuster began producing their *Little Golden Books*, which sold for 25 cents, and these became an important outlet for Donald, as did the *Top-Top Tales*, *Tell-a-Tales* and *Cozy Corner Books* series.

Of all Donald's book publishers, Whitman was the most prolific. The company's most-popular series were *Big Little Books* and *Better Little Books*. These child-sized chronicles cost 10 cents and measured $3\frac{3}{4} \times 4\frac{1}{2}$in (9.5 × 11.4cm), though they sometimes included up to 424 pages. Titles included such classics as *Donald*

Below: A defiant Donald graces the cover of the second Donald Duck book to be produced. It was published in 1936 by Grosset & Dunlap.

Below: Denuded of his usual sailor hat and sailor suit, Donald looks distinctly coy on the cover of this cut-out book, *Walt Disney's Donald Duck and Clara Cluck*. The book was probably published around 1939 in England.

Duck and Ghost Morgan's Treasure, published in 1946, and *Donald Duck and the Mystery of the Double X*, published in 1949. These two stories were reprints of Carl Barks comic books.

Donald was also marketed in numerous picture books, shape books (die-cut around the cover art), pop-up books, painting and coloring books. Like the cartoon shorts, these books had their heyday in the 1930s, 1940s and 1950s.

Many of the early Duck books contain exceptional graphics, which today are of great interest and appeal to collectors. Unlike the comic strips and comic books of the equivalent years, the artists of the frequently delightful, entertaining book illustrations remain for the most part unidentified. Probably the most comprehensive collection of these early volumes is held at the Walt Disney Archives at Burbank, California, where there are books and comic books in 35 languages from 46 countries. Some publications, especially those from prewar Europe, such as the annuals issued by the English publishers Dean & Son and Collins, are rare and full of graphic excitement.

Donald has appeared in a wide variety of publications, including painting and coloring books. Above: Donald gets to work with the paint pots himself on the title page of a painting book published by Grosset & Dunlap in 1936.

The story of *The Wise Little Hen* marked Donald's film debut. It also brought about the commencement of his remarkable career in comics. After the film's release in 1934, the story was run from September 16, 1935, for several months in the Sunday papers as one of Disney's *Silly Symphony* comic strips. Donald was obviously a success, for on August 30, 1936, the title panel wording was changed to *Silly Symphony featuring Donald Duck*. The comic strips were now written by Ted Osborne and drawn by Al Taliaferro.

By 1937, the words *Silly Symphony* had been dropped completely, and the panel read simply *Donald Duck*. The Nephews soon put in an appearance, but this time they were quickly sent home. There was even mention of their father — hospitalized as the result of one of their pranks. December 5, 1937, marked Donald's last appearance in the *Silly Symphony* Sunday strip.

As the star of his own Sunday color comic strip, Donald was established in a comfortable middle-class home. He was soon joined by family and friends who provoked domestic dramas, such as that shown here. This strip was published on February 25, 1940, and it marked the first appearance of the Nephews in the color comics.

DONALD DUCK

King Features syndicated the daily black-and-white Donald Duck strip from its first appearance in February 1938. The two strips shown above were published on April 11 and April 12, 1938.

On February 7, 1938, however, Donald became the star of his own black-and-white daily strip, syndicated by King Features. It was written by Bob Karp until July 1974 and drawn by Al Taliaferro until his death in 1969, a 31-year achievement exceeded only by Floyd Gottfredson of Mickey and Goofy fame. The same duo also produced Donald's own Sunday color strip, which first appeared on December 10, 1939, though Ted Osborne wrote some of the early story lines.

The strip stories were similar to those of Donald's contemporary shorts — domestic catastrophes interspersed with a few episodes involving mountain climbing or fishing trips. But they always stressed Donald's bad luck and worsening temper. In the strips, as well as in the films and books, Donald acquired a full complement of family, friends and neighbors. The Nephews arrived in Donald's daily strip life in 1938, and Gus appeared. Then on November 4, 1940, along came Daisy to drive him crazy. As his next-door neighbor, she became a strong factor in the strips.

Grandma Duck made her "daily" debut on September 27, 1943, and Professor Ludwig von Drake took time off from his television series to pay

unwelcome visits to both Sunday and daily strips in 1961. Scrooge did not join his comic strip family until 1960 in the Sunday strips and 1964 in the dailies, despite his creation by Carl Barks in 1947. The newspaper comics did not stress Scrooge's wealth as much as his role of "boss," wielding unimpeachable clout as head of the family.

Over the years, the humor of the Donald comic strips altered considerably. Early jokes were largely visual — Donald chased by seals, throttled by a rooster, bathing in a Police Department sidecar. Often there was no dialogue at all or the final panel was left silent to achieve full gag impact. However, wise-cracking, smart remarks and competitive verbal exchanges later became the norm. Take this typical example:

Donald: "I deserve a larger paycheck."

Scrooge: "I agree. Is 11 by 14 enough?"

Donald's highly successful comic strip career continues to this day.

In 1938 he entered yet another area of publishing, one which was eventually

Below: Yet more problems for Donald in these two daily black-and-white strips published on April 18 and April 19, 1938.

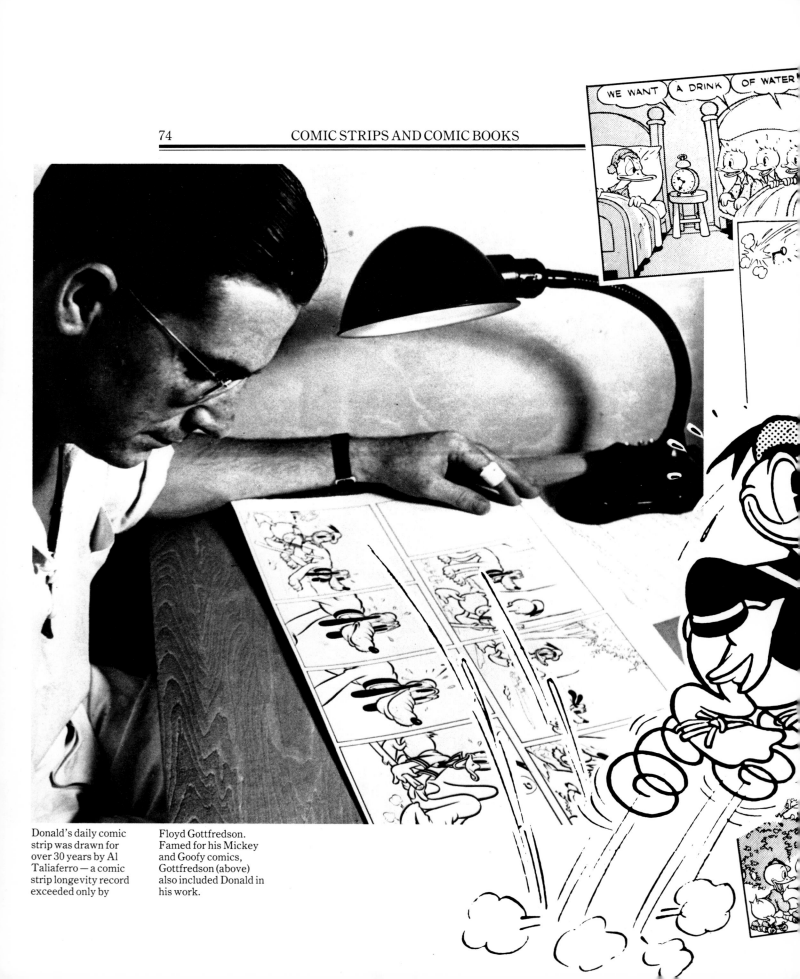

Donald's daily comic strip was drawn for over 30 years by Al Taliaferro — a comic strip longevity record exceeded only by Floyd Gottfredson. Famed for his Mickey and Goofy comics, Gottfredson (above) also included Donald in his work.

to project him into situations and places where no duck had ever gone before — the fantastic realms of the comic book. 1938 saw the rise of comic books as a great American phenomenon. With the first appearance of *Superman* that year, comic books became an overnight sensation. *Batman and Robin* appeared in 1939, *Captain Marvel* in 1940 and *Wonder Woman* in 1941. Disney quickly took advantage of the trend. In 1938, K. K. Publications produced a black-and-white Donald comic book with cardboard covers. Dell published a black-and-white comic book featuring Donald in 1940, and he was among the first Disney characters to appear in *Dell Color Comics* (No. 4,

published in February 1940). The first number of *Walt Disney's Comics and Stories*, published by Dell, appeared in October 1940 with Donald on the cover.

In 1942, Barks and Hannah were approached with the proposition of drawing and inking a Donald Duck comic book. With the Studio's permission, the team worked evenings and weekends on the project. It was natural that the "Duck Men" should gravitate toward what they knew best, so they reworked, possibly at Disney's suggestion, an unproduced film script. Bob Karp broke the story down into panels, and Barks and Hannah each did 32 of the 64 pages. The result was

The early black-and-white Donald strips stressed the Duck's bad luck and temper. Examples of his "true grit" were also included. The strips above were published on May 26 and April 6, 1938. The strip below appeared on May 27, 1938.

Many early Donald strips had little or no dialogue. Gags were based on Donald's irascible nature. The pictures usually spoke for themselves. Below: This Sunday strip — without dialogue — was published on December 29, 1940.

Dell Four Color Comics No. 9, *Donald Duck Finds Pirate Gold*. This is now a collector's item worth around $2,000 in 1984. Oddly, the cover artist is unknown. In 1943, Barks wrote and drew *Donald Duck and the Mummy's Ring* alone, but he did not do his first comic book cover until June 1948.

Barks started at the Disney Studio in 1935 as an in-betweener. But his great talent as a gag man and his special affinity for Donald ensured his transferral to the Story Department where he worked, mainly with Hannah, for 6½ years. His many film credits from this period include *Donald's Nephews* (1938)

and *Mr. Duck Steps Out* (1940).

During World War II Barks left the Disney Studio, intending to start a chicken ranch. But duck, not chicken, was to be his "meat." He subsequently became the most popular, prodigious Donald Duck comic book artist of all time. "I was a Duck man, not a Mouse man, but I was a Mouse man by personality," he used to say.

At the time of Barks' "retirement" from the Studio, Western Printing & Lithographing were looking for artists to provide material for their monthly *Comics and Stories* series. Barks completed a 10-page script sent him by Western, who were so impressed that they then had him begin both to write and to illustrate their

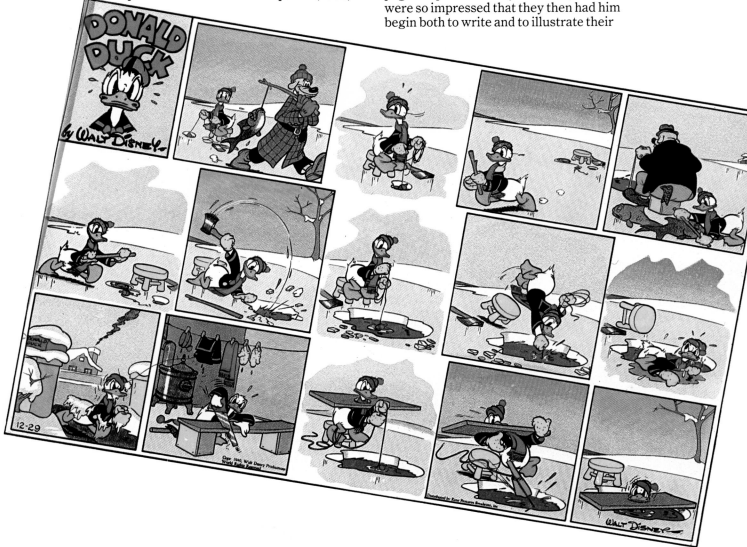

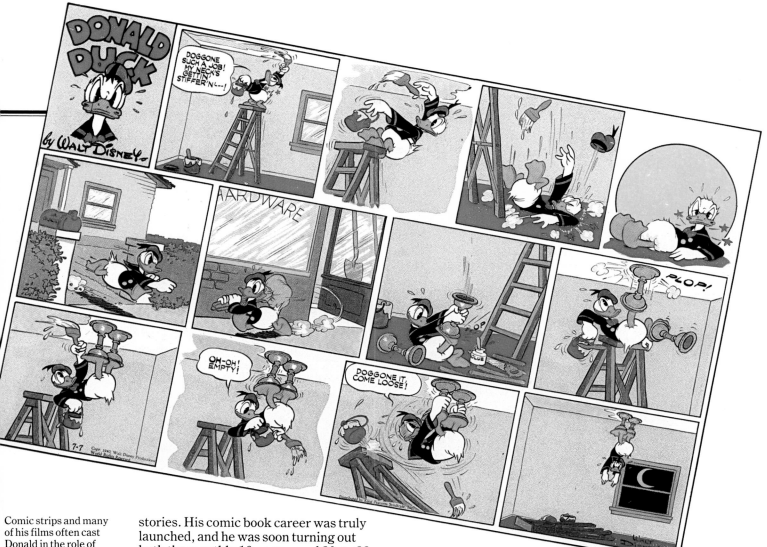

Comic strips and many of his films often cast Donald in the role of problem-solver. But his ingenuity frequently backfired, even in the most straightforward household chores. Above: Donald's attempt to paint a ceiling proves disastrous in this Sunday strip of July 7, 1940.

stories. His comic book career was truly launched, and he was soon turning out both the monthly 10-pagers and 20- to 32-page one-shots. In 1950, he drew, among others, a now standard model sheet entitled *How to Draw Donald Duck*. Prior to this reference, all comic artists had used Disney film animation model sheets.

In the early 1950s, Barks abandoned the 10-pagers and concentrated on Western's *Donald Duck* series and the new 25-cent comics. But readers complained about the change, so his story-art combination was reinstated in the monthlies. He went on to produce every Donald Duck story for *Walt Disney's Comics and Stories* for the next 13 years, until May 1964. Always prolific, in 1960 he produced 358 pages of artwork, 249 of text, 15 covers and 4 cover gags.

It was the longer comic books that provided the best scope for Barks' wild imagination. Donald's courage gradually became more important, and in the longer comics, Barks stressed the Duck's heroism. In the longer comics, Barks also made use of the exotic settings and costume dramas that were successful in other contemporary comic books. He infused them with myth, legend and his own special magic, broadening the stage for Donald's adventures. The super-heroes found themselves challenged by a duck.

The late 1940s brought a new emphasis on comedy or rather a blend of comedy and adventure. The early stories were founded on jokes or on the conflict between Donald and his Nephews. As Barks said, "Language is the key to personhood," and freed of his compulsory squawk, Donald was more able to articulate his thoughts and feelings. Perhaps this stress on the verbal accounts, more than anything, for Donald's transformation into the multidimensional, humanized duck he has become.

Barks' writing ability, as well as his draftsmanship, accounts for his appeal to both adults and children. He is a parodist and satirist, mixing the profound with the absurd, always ready to attack pomposity and self-importance and not without a certain cynical twist to his nature. He is obsessed with the power of money and luck, which he personifies in Scrooge and Gladstone. By forcing Donald to compete against this unconquerable combination,

Donald Duck Finds Pirate Gold (Dell Four Color Comics No. 9) was published in 1942. It was the first Donald comic book that the "Comic Book King" Carl Barks worked on. The workload was split between Barks and Jack Hannah. The duo had already collaborated for 6½ years as story men at the Disney Studio.

he emphasizes Donald's human failings and enhances his personhood. "In Barks' universe, to be human is to be victim; and Donald grows in humanity as he loses repeatedly to his kin," said Thomas Andrae and Geoffrey Blum in their 1983 essay, *A Question of Identity*.

The complex plots of the 32-page comic books required more characters, not just a vast *ambiance*. Like no one before him, Barks understood the potential of Huey, Dewey and Louie—after all, he had assisted at their "birth." Through their involvement with the Junior Wood-

In 1943, Carl Barks wrote and drew the classic comic book *Donald Duck and the Mummy's Ring* (Dell Four Color Comics No. 29). Though he worked solo on the book, Barks did not draw its cover.

The infamous Uncle Scrooge McDuck was created by Carl Barks in 1947. Scrooge subsequently became a hero in his own right and led Donald and the Nephews on the trail of many exotic and fantastic adventures. In 1952, Scrooge became the star of his own comic books, most of which were published under the Gold Key imprint, including the three shown here.

chucks, a gentle satire on the Boy Scouts, the Nephews acquired a fund of inexhaustible knowledge, which made them Donald's peers, if not his superiors. This was a new, highly successful treatment of the childhood fantasy of overcoming the parent.

Daisy was seldom used by Barks and certainly never developed, while Gladstone served mainly as a goad for Donald. It was Uncle Scrooge, Barks' greatest and best-loved creation, who became not only a fully rounded character, but served as instigator of adventures, taking Donald and the Nephews globe-trotting in quest of even greater riches. Through him, Barks achieved a unique mixture of geography and derring-do. Scrooge first appeared in 1947 in the comic book *Christmas on Bear Mountain*, but it was in *Letter to Santa* that he assumed his classic identity, both as miser and protagonist. In 1952, with the publication of *Only a Poor Old Man*, Scrooge became the star of his own comic book series. In this story, the old coot was rendered more sympathetic. The Scrooge comic book series was published under the Dell, then Gold Key, imprints.

Barks was "discovered" by collectors in 1959 and 1960. He retired in 1966, with over 500 comic book stories to his credit. But it was not until the 1970s that he really became a cult figure and the focus of the adulation of millions. Barks fan clubs sprang up all over the world. Many people sensed in his stories a complex, profound comment on human existence. One German club even developed this quest for meaning into a highly intellectualized game in which Scrooge's fortune was computed in Deutschmarks and a so-called "duck mile" was invented for measuring distances from Duckburg.

"One day, later, when we bomb ourselves silly and get dug up by scholars with spades, *The Best of Donald Duck* will be the *Hamlet* of its day. Nothing that complicated can be that simple. It's got to have a message or we're lost," wrote "B.E." in *Oz* magazine in 1963. Plainly, what we have here is a case of Barksmania.

After retiring from comic work, Barks' intention was to take up painting landscapes. But his fans would not stand for his attempted retirement. Nor, it seems, would Donald. A compromise was worked out, and Barks began immortalizing his creations with oil on canvas. He obtained permission from Disney to paint ducks. Between 1971 and 1976, he produced 122 paintings that range in size from 8×6in (20.3×15.2cm) to 18×24in (45.7×70cm). His paintings were published in 1981 by Another Rainbow Publishing in *The Fine Art of Walt Disney's Donald Duck*.

Based on his sustained output of paintings, Barks has also produced a series of lithographs in conjunction with Another Rainbow Publishing, a licensee of Walt Disney Productions. "*A 1934 Belchfire Runabout!*," shown on page 41, is his latest work. It is fourth in the lithograph series and his personal birthday tribute to Donald and the early world of Disney. Much sought-after by comic enthusiasts, his paintings and lithographs have become valuable collectors' items. Barks has truly gone from "Comic Book King" to "Duck Master."

Carl Barks wrote and drew the comic book *Donald Duck and the Golden Helmet* in 1952. When Barks retired from comic book work, he re-created many of his famous Donald Duck comic book covers as oil paintings. He produced this painting of *Donald Duck and the Golden Helmet* in 1972. It measures 20 × 16in (50 × 40cm).

Another Barks oil painting of one of his classic Donald comic book covers. The comic book *Donald Duck in Ancient Persia* was created by Barks in 1950. His painting of the same subject, shown here, was produced in 1971. It measures 20 × 16in (50 × 40cm). All the typical Barks motifs are present in it: Donald's rivalry with his Nephews, mythology, ancient lands and the quest for gold and adventure.

DUCKMANIA
MERCHANDISING DONALD

Right: This entertaining postcard was produced in Sweden. It is a near-copy of a Barks illustration in *Walt Disney's Comics and Stories* (No. 130), published in July 1951. The postcard artist added Mickey and Goofy in the background and the fish in the foreground. The card measures $3\frac{1}{2} \times 5\frac{1}{2}$ in (8.5 × 14cm).

Below: Donald and Mickey in a rowboat. This celluloid toy was made in the mid-1930s. Like many celluloid toys of the period, it was made in Japan. It measures 6in (15.2cm) long.

The great success of *The Wise Little Hen* in 1934 meant that Donald's image appeared almost immediately on a wide variety of merchandise. Disney already had an elaborate network of licensees who paid royalties to produce and sell Mickey Mouse products. By the time of Donald's debut, Kansas City ad man Herman "Kay" Kamen was representing the company among a large group of manufacturers. Thus, Donald's entry into the marketplace was greatly facilitated by

this established, flourishing merchandising system. The same firms that had so lucratively exploited Mickey Mouse, quickly welcomed Donald to their product lines.

Fisher Price Toys, the Ingersoll-Waterbury Clock Company, the Lionel Corporation, Knickerbocker Toys, Ohio Art, Seiberling Latex Products, Salem China and Whitman Publishing all introduced the new Disney character to their merchandise programs. By 1935, there were Donald Duck handkerchiefs, pull-toys, books, soap, neckties, card games and celluloid and bisque figures. The Donald of these products followed the physical form of the early Duck with long bill and neck and fat body. To indicate his mischievous nature, one of his eyes was usually closed in a wink.

Graphically stylized eyes were a

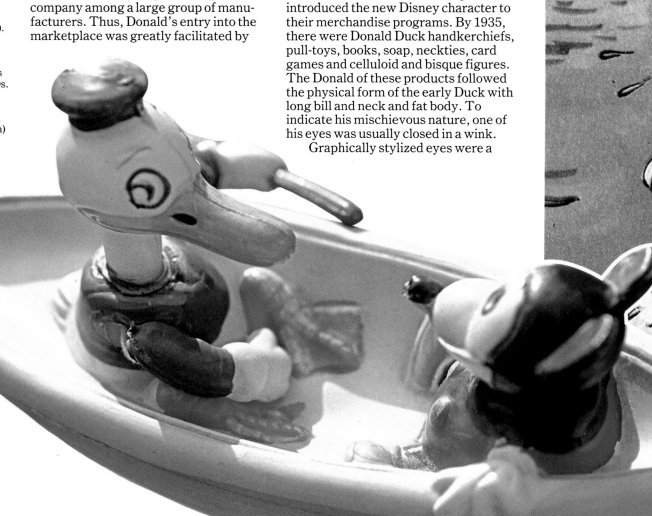

particular feature of many early celluloid Donalds, along with wind-up clockwork mechanisms which caused the body to agitate and the arms to wave. Such toys were made in Japan, like numerous other celluloid figures of the time.

Armies of ducks invaded retail stores throughout the world, and by 1936, one could purchase Duck jewelry, cereal bowls, pencil boxes, belts, toothbrushes, dolls, lamps and writing tablets. The Lionel Corporation produced an especially popular rail car featuring Donald and Pluto. It came complete with a circular 27in (68.5cm) track and a modest price tag of $1.25. The first Donald Duck watch was sold by Ingersoll in 1939.

Though Donald did well in the merchandise marketplace, his success never equalled that of Mickey, who found overwhelming commercial favor. Merchandise seems to have been Mickey's specialty, and from the beginning, Mickey toys, dolls, games and figurines vastly outnumbered similar items featuring Donald. Fewer Donald items were made during the vintage years of the 1930s, simply because Mickey was created several years before

Bottom left: Fisher Price Toys manufactured this wooden Donald pull-toy in the 1930s.

Left: Donald Duck as cowboy! Made during the 1930s by Knickerbocker Toys, this stuffed cloth Donald doll came complete with full cowboy regalia. It measures 13in (33cm) high.

Below: This Donald Duck savings bank anticipates Scrooge's obsession with money! Made from painted metal, it was produced in the mid-1930s. It measures 6½in (16.5cm) high.

The Lionel Corporation's Donald Duck rail car is shown here, complete with original box. It is one of the most famous Donald toys. Donald and Pluto are propelled in their rail car around the eight pieces of track that were supplied with this magnificent wind-up toy. A noisemaker contained in the toy's mechanism causes Donald to quack every time the car goes around the track. Manufactured in 1936, the rail car measures 10in (25.5cm) long.

Donald. Mickey appeared in 1928, and his toys appeared in 1930. Thus vintage Mouse merchandise had an advantage of more than four years. Also, Donald's unique charisma was probably not as easy to translate into static forms that gave little suggestion of his real vitality and flexibility. By contrast, Mickey's charm was primarily visual and symbolic so virtually anything sporting his image was guaranteed to sell. It is even possible that parents may have considered the temperamental Donald a poor role model for children and were not eager to introduce the ill-mannered fellow into their households.

Whatever the reasons, Donald's triumphs remained in film and print, mediums in which he could rely on his personality and where there was a story to make use of his wide range of emotions. For he is primarily a character, and this is the reason why the most interesting, sought-after Duck merchandise is that which captured Donald in an attitude — such as angry, mischievous, boisterous or whimsical — that exploited his personality and charm.

Collectors of Disney memorabilia divide Donald Duck merchandise into two periods — the long-billed Donald who dates from 1934 to 1937, and the short-

Below left: The American firm of Milton Bradley produced this Donald Duck poster paint set in 1938.

Below right: Ingersoll manufactured this Donald Duck pocket watch in 1939. Its launch marked the first appearance of Donald's image on a timepiece.

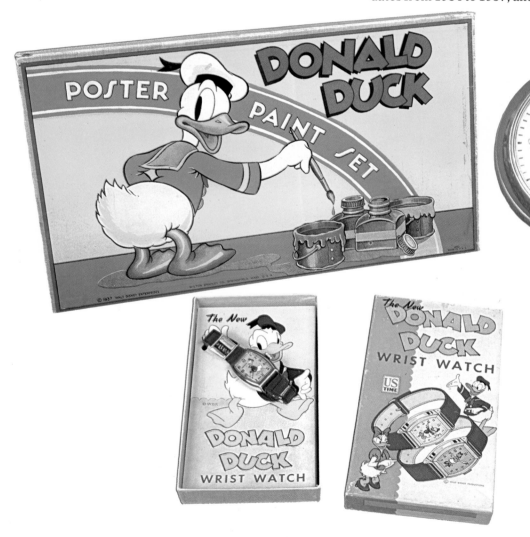

Left: Shown here with its original box, this Donald Duck wristwatch was manufactured by US Time in 1948. The famous Ingersoll-Waterbury Clock Company — which was taken over by US Time — had such a success with Mickey Mouse timepieces that the Donald watch was a natural development.

Donald is the only major Disney character ever featured on food products. In this 1953 photograph, Walt Disney and Donald promote a range of Donald Duck citrus juice products from Florida.

Right: David Niven, Ginger Rogers and numerous Donalds in *Bachelor Mother* (1939). The Duck toys include tinplate Donalds, made by Schuco, and fabric Donalds, made by Knickerbocker Toys. (Photograph: Courtesy of RKO General Pictures.)

Below: This contemporary Donald is a ''Bendy toy,'' made from rubber-coated wire. Bendy toys were first produced in London in 1946 by Charles and Harry Neufeld. They originally developed the Bendy process in jelly molds. Today, Bendy toys are made and sold worldwide.

billed, well-proportioned, post-1937 Duck we know today. Toy collectors prefer the earlier, long-billed Donald for his rarity value, while comic book enthusiasts go for the short-billed version, often referred to as the ''Barks Donald.'' The later Donald is unique among Disney characters in one area. During the 1940s and 1950s, Duck merchandising took a new, previously unexplored direction, and Donald began to be featured on a wide variety of food products. Soon Donald Duck bread, orange juice, pop corn, soda pop, rice and coffee were being sold. Advertising material, labels and packaging for these Duck comestibles have all become popular, though rare, collectors' items.

Not just the sole preserve of the American public, Donald merchandise has been marketed globally, appearing over the years in Britain, France, Italy, Denmark, Sweden, Japan, Australia, South America and elsewhere. Interestingly, little Donald merchandise was produced in Germany in the 1930s because Hitler, who considered Mickey Mouse a symbol of American decadence, banned the manufacture of all Disney items in 1935. Because the Duck did not make his debut until 1934, there were few prewar German Donald products other than the classic, long-billed squawking Duck, made by Schuco. Examples are shown with David Niven and Ginger Rogers in the *Bachelor Mother* film-still illustrated here. Activate the clockwork mechanisms, and these tin Donalds quiver and shake in their cloth sailor suits while squawking loudly in the very best Duck fashion.

Right: Pelham Puppets
made this Donald
puppet around 1939. It
measures 12in
(30.5cm) high.

FILMOGRAPHY

The following comprehensive filmography lists the shorts, features and commercial films in which Donald Duck has appeared over the last 50 years. The names of the directors of these productions are given in brackets.

Donald also appeared in a number of television shows between 1954 and 1963.

1934
The Wise Little Hen (Silly Symphony. Wilfred Jackson)
Orphan's Benefit (Mickey Mouse cartoon. Bert Gillett)
The Dognapper (Mickey Mouse cartoon. Dave Hand)

1935
The Band Concert (Mickey Mouse cartoon. Wilfred Jackson)
Mickey's Service Station (Mickey Mouse cartoon. Ben Sharpsteen)
Mickey's Fire Brigade (Mickey Mouse cartoon. Ben Sharpsteen)
On Ice (Mickey Mouse cartoon. Ben Sharpsteen)
Mickey's Polo Team (Mickey Mouse cartoon. Dave Hand)

1936
Orphan's Picnic (Mickey Mouse cartoon. Ben Sharpsteen)
Mickey's Grand Opera (Mickey Mouse cartoon. Wilfred Jackson)
Moving Day (Mickey Mouse cartoon. Ben Sharpsteen)
Alpine Climbers (Mickey Mouse cartoon. Dave Hand)
Mickey's Circus (Mickey Mouse cartoon. Ben Sharpsteen)
Donald and Pluto (Mickey Mouse cartoon. Ben Sharpsteen)

1937
Don Donald (Mickey Mouse cartoon. Ben Sharpsteen)
Magician Mickey (Mickey Mouse cartoon. Dave Hand)
Moose Hunters (Mickey Mouse cartoon. Ben Sharpsteen)
Mickey's Amateurs (Mickey Mouse cartoon. Pinto Colvig, Walt Pfeiffer, Ed Penner)
Modern Inventions (Mickey Mouse cartoon. Jack King)
Hawaiian Holiday (Mickey Mouse cartoon. Ben Sharpsteen)
Clock Cleaners (Mickey Mouse cartoon. Ben Sharpsteen)
Donald's Ostrich (Jack King)
Lonesome Ghosts (Mickey Mouse cartoon. Bert Gillett)

1938
Self Control (Jack King)
Boat Builders (Mickey Mouse cartoon. Ben Sharpsteen)
Donald's Better Self (Jack King)
Donald's Nephews (Jack King)
Mickey's Trailer (Mickey Mouse cartoon. Ben Sharpsteen)
Polar Trappers (Ben Sharpsteen)
Good Scouts (Academy Award nomination. Jack King)
The Fox Hunt (Ben Sharpsteen)
The Whalers (Mickey Mouse cartoon. Dick Huemer)
Donald's Golf Game (Jack King)

1939
Donald's Lucky Day (Jack King)
Hockey Champ (Jack King)
Donald's Cousin Gus (Jack King)
Beach Picnic (Clyde Geronimi)
Sea Scouts (Dick Lundy)
Donald's Penguin (Jack King)
The Autograph Hound (Jack King)
Officer Duck (Clyde Geronimi)
The Standard Parade (Standard Oil Company. Director unknown)

1940
The Riveter (Dick Lundy)
Donald's Dog Laundry (Jack King)
Tugboat Mickey (Mickey Mouse cartoon. Clyde Geronimi)
Billposters (Clyde Geronimi)
Mr. Duck Steps Out (Jack King)
Put-Put Troubles (Riley Thomson)
Donald's Vacation (Jack King)
Window Cleaners (Jack King)
Fire Chief (Jack King)
The Volunteer Worker (Community Chests and Councils, Inc. Riley Thomson)

1941
Timber (Jack King)
Golden Eggs (Wilfred Jackson)
A Good Time for a Dime (Dick Lundy)
The Nifty Nineties (Mickey Mouse cartoon. Riley Thomson)

Early to Bed (Jack King)
Truant Officer Donald (Academy Award nomination. Jack King)
Orphan's Benefit (Mickey Mouse cartoon, color remake. Riley Thomson)
Old MacDonald Duck (Jack King)
Donald's Camera (Dick Lundy)
Chef Donald (Jack King)
Mickey's Birthday Party (Mickey Mouse cartoon. Riley Thomson)
The Reluctant Dragon (Feature. Live Action Director: Alfred L. Werker. Cartoon Directors: Hamilton Luske, Jim Handley, Ford Beebe, Erwin Verity, Jasper Blystone)

1942
The Village Smithy (Dick Lundy)
Symphony Hour (Mickey Mouse cartoon. Riley Thomson)
Donald's Snow Fight (Jack King)
Donald Gets Drafted (Jack King)
Donald's Garden (Dick Lundy)
Donald's Gold Mine (Dick Lundy)
The Vanishing Private (Jack King)
Sky Trooper (Clyde Geronimi)
Bellboy Donald (Jack King)
The New Spirit (US Treasury Department. Wilfred Jackson and Ben Sharpsteen)
Donald's Decision (National Film Board of Canada. Ford Beebe)
All Together (National Film Board of Canada. Ford Beebe)

1943
Der Fuehrer's Face (Academy Award. Jack Kinney)
Donald's Tire Trouble (Dick Lundy)
Flying Jalopy (Dick Lundy)
Fall Out — Fall In (Jack King)
The Old Army Game (Jack King)
Home Defense (Jack King)
Saludos Amigos (Feature. Production Supervisor: Norman Ferguson. Sequence Directors: Bill Roberts, Jack Kinney, Hamilton Luske, Wilfred Jackson)

The Spirit of '43 (US Treasury Department. Jack King)

1944
Trombone Trouble (Jack King)
Donald Duck and the Gorilla (Jack King)
Contrary Condor (Jack King)
Commando Duck (Jack King)
The Plastics Inventor (Jack King)
Donald's Off Day (Jack Hannah)

1945
The Clock Watcher (Jack King)
The Eyes Have It (Jack Hannah)
Donald's Crime (Academy Award nomination. Jack King)
Duck Pimples (Jack King)
No Sail (Jack Hannah)
Cured Duck (Jack King)
Old Sequoia (Jack King)
The Three Caballeros (Feature. Production Supervisor/Director: Norman Ferguson. Sequence Directors: Clyde Geronimi, Jack King, Bill Roberts. *La Piñata* and *Baia*, shorts from *The Three Caballeros*, not released as separate films theatrically.)

1946
Donald's Double Trouble (Jack King)
Wet Paint (Jack King)
Dumb Bell of the Yukon (Jack King)
Lighthouse Keeping (Jack Hannah)
Frank Duck Brings 'Em Back Alive (Jack Hannah)

1947
Straight Shooters (Jack Hannah)
Sleepy Time Donald (Jack King)
Clown of the Jungle (Jack Hannah)
Donald's Dilemma (Jack King)
Crazy With the Heat (Charles Nichols)
Bootle Beetle (Jack Hannah)
Wide Open Spaces (Jack King)
Chip an' Dale (Academy Award nomination. Jack Hannah)
Fun and Fancy Free (Feature. Production Supervisor: Ben Sharpsteen. Live Action Director: William Morgan. Cartoon Directors: Jack Kinney, Bill Roberts, Hamilton Luske. *Mickey and the Beanstalk*, featurette from *Fun and Fancy*

Free, not released as a separate film theatrically.)

1948
Drip Dippy Donald (Jack King)
Daddy Duck (Jack Hannah)
Donald's Dream Voice (Jack King)
The Trial of Donald Duck (Jack King)
Inferior Decorator (Jack Hannah)
Soup's On (Jack Hannah)
Three for Breakfast (Jack Hannah)
Tea for Two Hundred (Academy Award nomination. Jack Hannah)
Melody Time (Feature. Production Supervisor: Ben Sharpsteen. Cartoon Directors: Clyde Geronimi, Wilfred Jackson, Hamilton Luske, Jack Kinney)

1949
Donald's Happy Birthday (Jack Hannah)
Sea Salts (Jack Hannah)
Winter Storage (Jack Hannah)
Honey Harvester (Jack Hannah)
All in a Nutshell (Jack Hannah)
The Greener Yard (Jack Hannah)
Slide, Donald, Slide (Jack Hannah)
Toy Tinkers (Academy Award nomination. Jack Hannah)

1950
Lion Around (Jack Hannah)
Crazy Over Daisy (Jack Hannah)
Trailer Horn (Jack Hannah)
Hook, Lion and Sinker (Jack Hannah)
Bee at the Beach (Jack Hannah)
Out on a Limb (Jack Hannah)

1951
Dude Duck (Jack Hannah)
Corn Chips (Jack Hannah)
Test Pilot Donald (Jack Hannah)
Lucky Number (Jack Hannah)
Out of Scale (Jack Hannah)
Bee on Guard (Jack Hannah)

1952
Donald Applecore (Jack Hannah)
Let's Stick Together (Jack Hannah)
Uncle Donald's Ants (Jack Hannah)
Trick or Treat (Jack Hannah)
Pluto's Christmas Tree (Mickey Mouse cartoon. Jack Hannah)

1953
Don's Fountain of Youth (Jack Hannah)
The New Neighbor (Jack Hannah)
Rugged Bear (Academy Award nomination. Jack Hannah)
Working for Peanuts (Jack Hannah)
Canvas Back Duck (Jack Hannah)

1954
Spare the Rod (Jack Hannah)
Donald's Diary (Jack Kinney)
Dragon Around (Jack Hannah)
Grin and Bear It (Jack Hannah)
Grandcanyonscope (Charles Nichols)
Flying Squirrel (Jack Hannah)

1955
No Hunting (Academy Award nomination. Jack Hannah)
Bearly Asleep (Jack Hannah)
Beezy Bear (Jack Hannah)
Up a Tree (Jack Hannah)
Lake Titicaca (Bill Roberts. Short from *Saludos Amigos* feature)
Blame it on the Samba (Clyde Geronimi. Short from *Melody Time* feature. Rereleased in 1965)

1956
Chips Ahoy (Jack Kinney)
How to Have an Accident in the Home (Charles Nichols)

1959
Donald in Mathmagic Land (Featurette. Supervising Director: Hamilton Luske)
How to Have an Accident at Work (Charles Nichols)

1961
Donald and the Wheel (Hamilton Luske)
The Litterbug (Hamilton Luske)

1965
Steel and America (American Iron and Steel Institute. Les Clark)

1966
Donald's Fire Survival Plan (Educational release. Les Clark)

1983
Mickey's Christmas Carol (Mickey Mouse featurette. Burny Mattinson)

BIBLIOGRAPHY

The following bibliography represents a small but classic selection of other publications on Donald Duck and the world of Disney.

Bailey, Adrian, *Walt Disney's World of Fantasy* (1982, Everest House, New York/Paper Tiger, London)

Barks, Carl, *Donald Duck–Best Comic* (1978, Abbeville Press, New York)

Barks, Carl, *The Fine Art of Walt Disney's Donald Duck* (1981, Another Rainbow Publishing, Scottsdale, Arizona)

Barrier, Michael, "Carl Barks and the Disney Ducks; the Lord of Quackly Hall" (June 1967, *Funnyworld* No. 6)

Barrier, Michael, *Carl Barks and the Art of the Comic Book* (1981, M. Lilien, New York)

Blitz, Marcia, *Donald Duck* (1979, Harmony Books, New York/New English Library, London)

Burnet, Dana, "The Rise of Donald Duck" (October 1935, *Pictorial Review*)

Boatner, E.B., "Carl Barks–from Burbank to Calisota" (1977, *The Comic Book Price Guide* No. 7, Harmony Books, New York)

Canemaker, John (Introduction), *Treasures of Disney Animation Art* (1982, Abbeville Press, New York)

Ciotti, Paul, "The Man Who Drew Ducks" (November 1977, *PSA California Magazine*)

Crowther, Bosley, "Dizzy Disney: 'The Three Caballeros'

Shows Brilliant Technique–But Is It Art?" (February 11, 1945, *New York Times*)

Daugherty, Frank, "How Donald Comes Out of the Paint Pots" (December 14, 1940, *Christian Science Monitor*)

Feild, Robert D., *The Art of Walt Disney* (1942/4, Macmillan, New York/Collins, London and Glasgow)

Finch, Christopher, *The Art of Walt Disney–From Mickey Mouse to the Magic Kingdoms* (1973, Harry N. Abrams, New York)

Gottfredson, Floyd (Introduction), *Walt Disney's Mickey Mouse–Best Comics* (1978, Abbeville Press, New York)

Hamilton, Bruce (Ed), *The Carl Barks Library of Walt Disney's Donald Duck* (1983, Another Rainbow Publishing, Scottsdale, Arizona)

Hiss, Tony and McClelland, David, "The Quack and Disney" (December 29, 1975, *The New Yorker*)

Holliday, Kate, "Donald Duck Goes to War" (September 1942, *Coronet*)

Korkis, Jim, "A Brief Look at the Films of Donald Duck" (September 1979, *The Rocket's Blast/Comicollector*)

Maltin, Leonard, *Of Mice and Magic: A History of American Animated Cartoons* (1980,

McGraw Hill, New York)

Munsey, Cecil, *Disneyana: Walt Disney Collectibles* (1974, Hawthorn, New York)

Shale, Richard, "Donald Duck Joins Up–The Walt Disney Studio during World War II" (Fall 1977, *Funnyworld* No. 17)

Smith, David R., "Donald Duck: This is Your Life" (July 1984, *Starlog* No. 84)

Spicer, Bill, "A Visit with Carl Barks" (July 1971, *Graphic Story World* No. 2)

Summer, Edward, "Of Ducks and Men; Carl Barks Interviewed" (Spring 1981, *Panels* No. 2)

Thomas, Frank and Johnston, Ollie, *Disney Animation–The Illusion of Life* (1981, Abbeville Press, New York)

Thompson, Helen G., "Wanna Fight?" (May 1936, *Stage*)

Tobin, Richard, "The Rise of Donald Duck" (January 12, 1936, *New York Herald Tribune*)

Wagner, Dave, "Donald Duck: An Interview" (1973, *Radical America* No. 7)

"The Ascendancy of Mr. Donald Duck" (June 23, 1940, *New York Times*)

"D. Duck–a Reappraisal", signed B. E. (January 1967, *Oz* magazine. Reprint from May 1963)

DUCK LANGUAGE

The following list of "Practical Duck Expressions" is taken from a Disney Studio's internal information sheet issued around 1939. All these phrases "have been tested for clarity and we know they are understandable." They are also some of the most classic, entertaining and typical examples of the best of "Duck Dialogue."

Stop jittering, will ya!
You give me the jitters!
A good bath — that's what you need!
He'll go for this — absolutely!
Hey — what's the big idea?
Strategy, that's it — I'll try strategy!
You're goin' to get a bath — a real bath!
Well — I'll be...!
Oh, boy — it's a cinch!
Why don't you cooperate?
I'll fix him!
I've got him where I want him.
It's stuck!
What a peculiar situation!
This is very, very funny!
Aw nuts!
Nice kitty, do your stuff!
Here he comes.
What's goin' on here?
Let me go!
Let me out of here!
You can't do this to me.
The dirty dog!
He's one of the family, allright!
Such ignorance!
I've got it!
I'll get rid of him.
What shall I do?
Oe — Oh — what's this?
Scram, you doggone pest!
The very idea, getting into my food!
Now let me see...
Directions — phooey!
Just leave it to your Uncle Donald!
Nope, that ain't right — uh-uh!
So — you're going to be obstinate, un?
Come on — open up.
I'll open you up if it's the last thing I do.
Are you back again?
Can you imagine that?
Put those down!
Come back you!
This is a fine situation.

This is a fine how-do-you-do.
This is a fine predicament.
Now I've got him where I want him.
Get away from that food!
Am I mortified!
Making a sap out of me.
Where do you think you're going?
Well, well, you don't say!
How about another smack!
What a woman!
There's something screwy about this!
I've got to get rid of those kids.
Here, boys — go get some ice cream.
How about a little kiss?
Did you say something?
You be careful!
How sweet of you!
For me?
I'll be right back.
What are you trying to do?
Now for a perfect day of rest!
Now for a perfect day of relaxation!
Are you insinuating?
Oh — what an appetite!
Cut it out!
Absolutely exasperating!
All right! All right!
Beat it! Scram!
Beat it! Scat!
Disgusting!
Exasperating!
Get a load o' this!
Get goin'!
Get outa here! Scram!
Get me outa this!
Gimme that!
G'wan! Scram!
Hot stuff! Hot stuff!
Hey!
Hi, toots!
I'll assassinate you!
I got him! I got him!
I'll get ya!

I'll be doggoned!
I'll tear you apart!
My! My!
No respect for human body!
Now I lay me down to sleep...
Bu... Bu... (scared)
Oh, boy! Am I hungry!
Oh, boy! What a setup!
Okay!
Okay, sourpuss!
Oh, boy!
Oh, boy! Oh, boy!
Oh-oh!
Phooey!
Positively disgusting!
Shut up!
So!
So...monkey business!
Scram...you...!
See? Nothing to it!
Shake a leg!
That's very, very considerate of you...
This is a fine kettle of fish!
That's the last straw!
There's nothing to it!
That'll hold ya!
That's gratitude for ya!
This is too much!
This needs some scientific strategy!
That's a dirty trick!
Watch this...I'll show ya something!
Watch this...I'll show ya how to do it!
What's the big idea!
Watch me...I'll show ya!
Well...I'll be a son of a gun!
What thuh...!
What a____! What a____!
Well, can you imagine that!
You dummy!
You doggone rubbernecks!
You doggone windbag!
You robbers!
You big palooka!